"I have known Pastor Mi[k] have watched firsthand how his love for Jesus and his heart for the lost and hurting in the world have driven his ministry. He lives just as he writes. His desire is to see those who don't know Jesus come to a saving faith in a loving God. When the heart of an evangelist meets a deep passion for Scripture, you get this book. It is a great read for those who have never walked inside a church, as well as those who have grown up in a church. It asks questions pastors and leaders get all the time, yet answers them with a caring pastor's heart."

—Jeff Ludington,
author of *Frustrated: How the Bible Resolves Life's Tough Questions;* Lead Pastor, Generations Church

"I've been a pastor for 27 years, and invariably am asked many spiritual questions. I always enjoy the questions I get, and I'm not bothered when people ask tough questions or raise dilemmas they're facing. In fact, I love that people are curious and want to learn enough to ask, and I'm honored to be able to answer people's questions, especially questions about faith. It's when people go through difficult experiences or see an injustice around them that they're spurred on to deep questions. Those questions deserve an answer, and the good news is that the Bible can answer a lot of people's deep questions. I'm so glad to see Mike has decided to write a book tackling some of the questions that people in our day are asking. I've known Mike for a number of years. He's preached at my church, and each time he's preached my people have reported to me how much they have loved Mike's teaching, how his messages challenged them to take action in their lives to follow God more boldly. Mike is a great communicator, he's passionate about his faith, he's a lifelong learner, he thinks deeply about the things he preaches and teaches about, and he cares about his listeners and desires for them to fall more deeply in love with our Savior Jesus Christ. You'll discover these tremendous qualities about Mike as you read this book, but you'll also discover how wonderful the Bible is in dealing with the real, tough issues we all face every day. This is why the Apostle Paul was never ashamed of the gospel of God: he knew it was the power of God for the salvation of everyone who believes, and he knew in this gospel a righteousness from God had been revealed in Jesus Christ (Rom. 1:16–17). Paul was not ashamed because he knew the gospel was good, powerful, true, and able to transform lives. You can bring your really tough questions to this gospel! So, get ready to encounter God's truth in these pages, and it's my prayer that he will not only answer your questions but draw you closer to himself."

—Ned Beadel,
Pastor Emeritus, Desert Winds Community Church;
Director of Church Health, Classis of California

"Mike Larsen is a friend of mine and one of the best men I know to tackle some of the subject matter he does in this book. Mike's heart in writing this truly bears his pastoral heart for people and his desire to be true to the words of Scripture. His writing is personal, heartfelt, and biblically thought-provoking."

—**Mike Gunn,**
Pastor, Anchor Community Church

"Confusion and doubts to unanswered questions cloud the mind and distract the soul. Pursuing thoughtful, biblical, and loving answers clears your path to enjoying God. Mike Larsen is a faithful and loving pastor and theologian who answers important questions we ask and have been asked. This book will equip you with biblical truth and Christlike compassion, which are both necessary. Read it, meditate on Scripture, and discuss it with others asking these questions in their minds."

—**P. J. Tibayan,**
Pastor, Bethany Baptist Church

"*Thanks for Asking* is a great reminder of how special and timeless God's word is and how the Bible transcends time and is as powerful today as it has ever been. Mike Larsen has done a marvelous job of pointing us to many answers in the Bible for today's infinite questions and challenges. Every time I had to put it down, I found myself intrigued about what answers were coming next. I'm looking forward to seeing answers to more questions in future editions of this book."

—Juan Garza,
Vice President, Englander Knabe & Allen;
Councilman, City of Bellflower

"What I love most about Mike's book is that it is written not from an academic to academics, but from a pastor to his people (even 10-year-old boys!). This is real-life ministry, and Mike does a great job answering honest questions honestly, biblically, and simply. He doesn't just answer questions, though—He shows how Jesus and the gospel provide the ultimate answer to all of our questions, and if you can get from dinosaurs to the gospel, that's a win. This book is simply doing what God told us to do: love people."

—Brett Visk,
Lead Pastor, Mere Church

"This book is excellent. I read it in one sitting. Great stories. Solidly biblical. Practical and 100% gospel-oriented. Well done, my friend!"

—Tom Hocking,
Senior Pastor, Bellflower Brethren Church

"Right from the opening of this book, Pastor Mike faces head-on the questions we all have asked at some point in our lives. This book stares right in the face of what I call the "Pink Elephants in the Room": questions that many, if not all, pastors have to answer in this world. Mike takes on those topics, addressing them with the lens of the gospel, from suffering, to alcohol, to dinosaurs, and beyond. It is refreshing to hear a pastor lean into the very places where the world is looking for answers from the church. This book will leave you wanting to search the Scriptures even more, opening up areas in your own life where you have avoided seeking answers."

—Pete Watts,
author of *Prodigal Father*; Regional Vice President, World Impact; Lead Pastor, The Rock Church

THANKS FOR ASKING

EQUIPPING GOD'S PEOPLE WITH ANSWERS TO LIFE'S TOUGH QUESTIONS

MIKE LARSEN

FOREWORD BY DAVE KRAFT

LUCIDBOOKS

THANKS FOR ASKING

Equipping God's People with Answers to Life's Tough Questions
Copyright © 2018 by Mike Larsen

Published by Lucid Books in Houston, TX
www.LucidBooksPublishing.com

eISBN-10: 1-63296-180-6
eISBN-13: 978-1-63296-180-8
ISBN-10: 1-63296-179-2
ISBN-13: 978-1-63296-179-2

TABLE OF CONTENTS

FOREWORD

Asking questions is a part of life. Even before children begin to talk, questions are forming in their little brains. Once they can talk in complete sentences, the questions seem to never end: Why do I have to go to bed? Why can't I go out and play? Why can't I touch the stove, hit my sister, put my finger in the light socket? What will happen if I (fill in the blank)? Why do I have to do my homework? Why are vegetables good for you? If you are a parent, you know what I mean.

As we get older and think about spiritual matters, the questions change and become more serious. How do I know the Bible can be trusted? If there is a God, why is there so much suffering in the world? Why is Jesus the only way?

It seems that many if not most of our questions have to do with why.

Developing good answers to relevant and important questions is always of tremendous help. In this book,

Pastor Mike Larsen takes on nine questions that were submitted by people in the church he pastors. They are all great questions that many people have asked at some time. As I read, I was impressed with the insightful answers to these oft-posed questions.

All of us, to some degree or another, wrestle with questions whose answers can help us continue to grow, appreciate the wise God we serve, and be of help to those held back because of unanswered or inadequately answered questions.

I recommend this book. I am confident you will find a few questions for which you are seeking answers and that you very well might know someone who has some of the same questions.

Dave Kraft
Pastor, Author, and Seminar Leader

ACKNOWLEDGMENTS

God knew that it is not good for me to be alone. I thank God for blessing me with my best friend, the love of my life: my wife, Sheila. She has believed and supported all my crazy dreams, which included writing this book. Second only to Christ, Sheila is the greatest gift that God has ever given me. She is my world, my inspiration, and the motivation for everything I do; and I dedicate this book to her. To all my amazing kids: you are a blessing and a gift from God. I hope and pray that one day you can read this book and understand why I have devoted so much of my life to serving Jesus. I'd like to thank my parents, grandparents, in-laws, brothers, aunts, uncles, cousins, nieces, and nephews, who have supported and encouraged me throughout my career. I look forward to discussing this book with you and helping you answer any questions you might have. A special thanks to Milt and Carol, Chris and Nichole, Tim and Jamie, Glen and Hilda, Larry and Jessica, Jeff and Anita, Dan and Lindy, Jeff and Lisa, Vinnie and Sherri, Eric and Jen, Greg and Mary, Danny and Lisa, and Kelly and Angela. You have modeled what it means to be a Christian. I treasure our friendship and I thank you for blessing and enriching my life. To my amazing church family: this book would not exist without you. Thanks for asking. Soli Deo Gloria.

Love, Grace, and Peace,

Mike Larsen

INTRODUCTION

One of my top 10 movies of all time has to be *A Few Good Men*, starring Jack Nicholson as Col. Nathan R. Jessup and Tom Cruise as Lt. Daniel Kaffee. In the movie, Col. Jessup orders a code red, which leads to Private Santiago's untimely death. If you saw the movie, you've probably never forgotten the scene in the courtroom where Lt. Kaffee presses Col. Jessup for a confession. Pridefully, Colonel Jessup asks Kaffee, "You want answers?" Kaffee responds, "I think I'm entitled to them!" Then Jessup fires back, "You want answers?!" to which Kaffee shouts, "I want the truth!" Private Santiago's life had been tragically cut short, and the family needed to know the truth.

Why does God allow suffering? Why am I here? Why do I exist? Over my years as a pastor, I've heard some tough questions asked about the Bible and about God. These were hard questions that the people in my church had, and these were also difficult questions that they had heard from people they encountered.

They needed answers.

To help equip our church to be on mission, our pastoral team solicited questions from our church family about faith, people, and life. The text in 1 Peter 3:15 became our guidepost for the message series: *"But in your hearts revere Christ as Lord. Always be prepared to give an answer to everyone who asks you to give the reason for the hope that you have. But do this with gentleness and respect"* (NIV).

This message series would prove to be inspired by God. We asked, and many questions were submitted. Why do bad things happen? What does the Bible say about homosexuality? Our church had so many questions for God, and we knew that others did, too.

If you have questions but are struggling to find the right answers, *Thanks for Asking* is the perfect place to start. This practical, approachable resource will help guide you to find solid, biblical answers to your questions.

In his Word, God speaks authoritatively and directly on certain subjects, giving us clear answers to life's pressing questions. There are, however, subjects about which God did not explicitly inform us. I believe this is because God's intent for the Bible is not to answer every question or resolve every debate. Even though there is not a clear answer to every question in life, the Bible is full of experiences that inform us directly and indirectly, helping us answer our questions. So, as we dive into the depths of Scripture, we can intelligently answer many of life's questions without contradicting or manipulating God's Word or deviating from his intent. There will be other times when we find that God is silent. And where he is silent, we have to be content to not have an answer. We have to believe and trust that if knowing meant survival in this life, then God would've told us. My hope and prayers are threefold. First, I hope and pray that these answers strengthen your faith in God and his life-giving Word. Second, I hope and pray this book will help you see how relevant God's Word is for our generation and the next. Finally, I hope and pray this book will help equip you to be on a mission, sharing your faith with the people God has placed in your life who need the real hope that comes from knowing Jesus Christ as Savior and Lord.

Take a step of faith, and pray this prayer with me:

Jesus, open our minds and hearts to hear and see you in a way that we have never seen you before. God, give us the faith to believe and trust your holy Word when you have spoken directly and to the point. Where you are not clear, please give us the wisdom to come to intelligent, biblical, rational conclusions that would not contradict your holy Word. And give us the humility to be silent where you, Lord, are silent. Grow us in our understanding that we may be equipped to give an answer for the hope we have in you, Jesus. We do all this for your glory Jesus and for our good of all people. Amen.

1

WHY DO BAD THINGS HAPPEN?

Let not your hearts be troubled. Believe in God; believe also in me . . . Peace I leave with you; my peace I give to you. Not as the world gives do I give to you. Let not your hearts be troubled, neither let them be afraid. You heard me say to you, "I am going away, and I will come to you." If you loved me, you would have rejoiced, because I am going to the Father, for the Father is greater than I. And now I have told you before it takes place, so that when it does take place you may believe. I will no longer talk much with you, for the ruler of this world is coming. He has no claim on me, but I do as the Father has commanded me, so that the world may know that I love the Father. Rise, let us go from here . . . I have said these things to you, that in me you may have peace. In the world you will have tribulation. But take heart; I have overcome the world.

John 14:1, 27–31; 16:33

Have you ever experienced a truly peaceful moment? Think about that snapshot of life when you realized all was right with the world. Maybe it was a great meal. Maybe you were with someone you loved in a picturesque setting without a care in the world.

By God's grace, Sheila and I were fortunate enough to take some time off recently. We chose Sedona, Arizona, and now Sheila and I have a favorite vacation spot. Sedona is a desert town surrounded by beautiful red-rock buttes, steep canyon walls, and pine tree forests. We planned our trip in March, which meant spring had just sprung, and everything was in bloom. The vivid green vegetation contrasted against the red landscape, and the temperature never rose above 79 degrees the entire weekend. We hiked up a trail that led us to the base of a butte called Bell Rock. We hiked up Bell Rock and when we reached the top, we took a moment to admire the view of the valley below. It was by far the most beautiful landscape I had ever seen. It was so peaceful. It felt like I was looking at a painting. The crystal blue sky was punctuated by perfectly placed white clouds that lay atop a majestic red-rock valley. I was in the most beautiful place I had ever seen, with my best friend.

At that moment, I thought to myself, "This is what heaven must be like." I cherished that moment, and I wish there were more moments like that. I think we all wish we could capture and prolong these kinds of moments. Eventually though, the vacation is over, and it's time to go home where we have to face the realities of life. All of us have these peaceful moments, and we can thank God for them. But we also live in the reality that life is not always peaceful. Sadly, tragedies can come when we least expect them. No one is immune from sickness, disaster, financial trouble, hardships, or relationship strain. It's not a question of "if" life troubles will come, but "when" troubles come, and we all ask ourselves, "Why?"

The Goodness of Creation

Imagine that you could fly 30,000 feet above the storyline of creation in Genesis and see it in one big sweep. What you would see is a beautiful, harmonious creation. Remember my "taste of heaven" from earlier? Now, recall your taste of heaven. Each of those snapshots is a great way to imagine how all things were good as God created them. In Genesis 1, we read that the creator God spoke all things into existence and that he created this world in a perfect state and declared all of creation good. The weather was good, and the earth was green and flourishing. Everything was right with the world.

Next, we're introduced to the creation of mankind. Recall that on each day of creation, God said it was good. His crowning achievement of creation was mankind, and it wasn't until that sixth day of creation that God said his creation was *very good* (Gen. 1:31). Unlike the rest of creation, human beings were made in the image and likeness of God. This means that male and female are able to resemble God in character, in relationship, in speech, and in actions.

Next, Genesis 2 takes us from the 30,000-foot view and brings us in closer, face-to-face with God's creation.

In this scene, we meet Adam and Eve. God formed Adam from the dirt of the ground, and he breathed the breath of life into Adam's lungs. God then put Adam in the garden to tend to it and gave him permission to eat from any tree in the garden with the exception of the *"tree of the knowledge of good and evil"* (Gen. 2:9).

In this scene, Adam enjoyed an unbroken relationship with God and was asked to trust, in faith, that what God says is good and true. Here, we see that true love for God is a choice, demonstrated through faith. God is determined to do good to those who love and trust him in faith. This is God's design for every relationship. Because God loved Adam, he warned him of the consequence of sin, which is death. But the tree of the knowledge of good and evil isn't the only tree in the garden. More importantly, in the middle of the garden is the tree of life.

The tree of life is the symbolic reminder of God's purpose for humanity; it is a picture of God's grace on display. It shows us that God is the giver of all life, truth, flourishing, and purpose. Through no power of their own, Adam and Eve become living and breathing beings, which shows us that life itself is a gift of God's grace. In the beginning, this is the environment Adam and Eve lived in. They had perfectly functioning bodies and breath in their lungs. And as a way to reflect himself, God invited Adam and Eve—and invites us—to experience the blessing of bringing life into the world. This is, in part, what it means to be made in the likeness of God as co-creators with God. God created Adam and Eve to be fruitful so that the glory and goodness of God would multiply through them.

God gave man dominion over the earth and the blessing of fruitfulness to fill the earth with more of God's people. Then, God gave Adam and Eve the gift of each other in marriage. As it says in Genesis 2:24–25, *"Therefore a man shall leave his father and his mother and hold fast to his wife, and they shall become one flesh. And the man and his wife were both naked and were not ashamed."*

In God's goodness and grace, he provided everything necessary for Adam and Eve to live and flourish and accomplish their purpose, which was to be fruitful and multiply. Through no power of their own, but because of the loving and gracious gift of God, Adam and Eve had every opportunity for a lifetime of love, fellowship, and intimacy with one another and with God. The Hebrew word *shalom*, which means peace, sums up the picture of God's creation. The earth was filled with God's *shalom*, the kind of peace where everything was working the way God had intended. But something went terribly wrong in Genesis 3, and ever since, humankind has been asking the questions such as, "Why do bad things happen? Why is there suffering?"

Each of us, in various ways, will ask the question, "Why do bad things happen?" It's the question on the heart of every person who has ever experienced tragedy, war, sickness, pain, suffering, injustice, evil, and death. This question often occurs to us when we're sick or a loved one is sick. In 2014, my dad was diagnosed with bladder cancer. This wasn't an infection remedied by taking antibiotics and drinking lots of water—it was cancer! To understand what was going on with his body, he had to submit to the authority of a doctor who could tell him what was wrong. This is true for us. We need to know the truth of our condition because the truth will set us free. We don't need to put Band-Aids on problems, and we can't put infernos out with garden hoses. Dad couldn't treat his cancer by drinking lots of water. Knowing the truth of the situation (that he had cancer) led my dad to seek proper treatment. By God's grace, my dad is doing better now.

We have to deal with this question of why bad things happen with the same sort of seriousness. When we get sick, we want to know why. When our relationship with God is broken, we also need to know why. This is what makes Genesis 3 one of the most important chapters in the Bible. It is so important because it explains why bad things happen in the world. But more importantly, it also declares the remedy.

In Genesis 2, God says all of his creation is very good, and the world was full of his peace. Then in Genesis 3, God reveals to us how everything went bad! This is where we can begin to answer this question. Once we know the cause of our problem (like my dad), then we can seek out the proper solution. Here, we will pick up the story about when sin (the problem) entered the world, and later on we'll consider the solution.

Now the serpent was more crafty than any other beast of the field that the Lord God had made. He said to the woman, "Did God actually say, 'You shall not eat of any tree in the garden'?" And the woman said to the serpent, "We may eat of the fruit of the trees in the garden, but God said, 'You shall not eat of the fruit

of the tree that is in the midst of the garden, neither
shall you touch it, lest you die.'"

Gen. 3:1–3

Satan slithers into the garden and for the first time
Adam and Eve's faith was put to the test. First, Satan
put doubt in Eve's mind and suggested God was
lying to them. Then, he minimized the consequence of
disobeying God. Here is exactly what he said: *"You will*
not surely die. For God knows that when you eat of it your
eyes will be opened, and you will be like God, knowing good
and evil" (Gen. 3:4–5).

Satan has been using these two tactics ever since. We
often don't see Satan's cunning in the moment, but we
can see it after we've made a mistake, right? Have you
ever known God's will, but then knowingly disobeyed
his Word? We don't always understand in the moment
what's happening, but after our world falls apart, we can
often trace things back to that moment of disobedience.

Eve was faced with either putting her trust in Satan
or in God's loving and graceful warning that eating from
this tree is deadly. Love and obedience are a choice. God
gave Adam and Eve the choice to love him by obeying
him. God gave them permission to eat from any tree in
the garden with the exception of one. If they disobeyed
God, then the consequence would be death.

The final temptation came when Satan promised that
they had nothing to lose by disobeying God. Instead,
he implied that their lives would be even better because
then they could be like God. They were tempted and
began considering that maybe they didn't need God

after all. They could be their own gods, living under their own rule, and making their own decisions. What was there to lose? The story continues:

> *So when the woman saw that the tree was good for food, and that it was a delight to the eyes, and that the tree was to be desired to make one wise, she took of its fruit and ate, and she also gave some to her husband who was with her, and he ate. Then the eyes of both were opened, and they knew that they were naked. And they sewed fig leaves together and made themselves loincloths.*
>
> Gen. 3:6–7

By eating of the tree of the knowledge of good and evil, Eve chose pride over humility. She put her faith in Satan, the father of lies, instead of God, the Father of life. Tragically, Adam sat quietly by, failing to trust in God and protect his wife. Instead, Adam joined his wife by eating from the tree. Their eyes were suddenly open to the reality of what they had done, and immediately they felt the effects and consequences of their sin. For the first time, they felt guilt and shame, which led them to run and hide from God.

> *And they heard the sound of the LORD God walking in the garden in the cool of the day, and the man and his wife hid themselves from the presence of the LORD God among the trees of the garden. But the LORD God called to the man and said to him, "Where are you?" And he said, "I heard the sound of you in the garden, and I was afraid, because I was naked, and I hid myself."*

He said, "Who told you that you were naked? Have you eaten of the tree of which I commanded you not to eat?" The man said, "The woman whom you gave to be with me, she gave me fruit of the tree, and I ate." Then the LORD God said to the woman, "What is this that you have done?" The woman said, "The serpent deceived me, and I ate." The LORD God said to the serpent, "Because you have done this, cursed are you above all livestock and above all beasts of the field; on your belly you shall go, and dust you shall eat all the days of your life. I will put enmity between you and the woman, and between your offspring and her offspring; he shall bruise your head, and you shall bruise his heel." To the woman he said, "I will surely multiply your pain in childbearing; in pain you shall bring forth children. Your desire shall be for your husband, and he shall rule over you." And to Adam he said, "Because you have listened to the voice of your wife and have eaten of the tree of which I commanded you, 'You shall not eat of it,' cursed is the ground because of you; in pain you shall eat of it all the days of your life; thorns and thistles it shall bring forth for you; and you shall eat the plants of the field. By the sweat of your face you shall eat bread, till you return to the ground, for out of it you were taken; for you are dust, and to dust you shall return."

Gen. 3:8–19

The Consequences of Sin

The consequence of Adam and Eve's disobedience was death, and that has had a tremendous impact on humanity and the world ever since.

13

Because sin entered the world, we can expect that our perfect and peaceful moments of life (such as when you are on vacation) are often the very opposite of real life. God's good creation and relationships, which were meant for flourishing, wholeness, love, and joy have been thrown into chaos as shown in the nearby table of opposites. Instead of life, we have death. Instead of peace, we have war. Instead of worship, we have rebellion. Instead of faith, we have doubt, and so on.

Life	Death
Worship	Rebellion
Faith	Doubt
Trust	Fear
Love	Hate
Responsibility	Blame Shifting
Intimacy	Separation
Humility	Pride
Generosity	Greed
Peace	War
Joy	Pain
Health	Sickness

At this point in the story, if you were God, what would you do? Would your initial response be an act of grace? Would you require some kind of payback for the wrong committed? Would you call the police or file a lawsuit? In this instance of disobedience, rebellion, and betrayal, how would you respond? It is easy to understand that there should be consequences for Adam and Eve's actions. It would actually be irresponsible if there were no consequences for sin. What's hard for us to fully grasp is how God responded to sin.

The Surprise of God's Grace

If we're honest, when we're wronged, our response is not to offer grace. But what did God do? First, he pursued Adam and Eve and mourned over what they had done. He then turned to Satan and cursed him. Then in Genesis 3:15, God offered Adam and Eve hope. Theologians and Bible nerds call this the "protoevangelium"—the first gospel. God promises that Jesus will come to crush the head of Satan and bring salvation to his people. Then, God went out of his way to cover their shame by sacrificing the first animal, stripping them of their own efforts to cover their shame with fig leaves. In this, God showed that their efforts to cover their guilt and shame would never work. Fig leaves were not sufficient. The consequence of sin was death, so something had to die. God in his grace, came to their rescue and provided them the first sacrifice for sin. This sacrifice would be the first of many, done in faith, pointing to the final sacrifice that God would provide through his son, Jesus.

The beauty of the first gospel is that God doesn't give Adam and Eve what they deserve for disobedience. Instead, God takes it upon himself to save his people. The same is true for us. He does this through Jesus Christ, who the Apostle Paul calls a second Adam (Rom. 5:12–19). Unlike the first Adam, Jesus was completely faithful to God. Jesus suffered and died as a holy and perfect sacrifice for God's people. In his book *Counterfeit Gospels*,

Trevin Wax says, "Our loving Creator who rightly shows Himself to be wrathful toward our sin is determined to turn the evil and suffering in our lives into good."[1] When we put our faith and trust in God's son, we are forgiven of our sins and now, by the grace of God through Jesus, the faithful have access to the presence of God—his wisdom, his power, and eternal life. The Bible says those who are united to Christ by faith are born again, forgiven of all sin, and given a new chance to live as God originally intended. We read in Colossians that we are to *put on the new self, which is being renewed in knowledge after the image of its creator* (Col. 3:10).

Because of Jesus and by his Spirit, we are able to live redeemed lives as God had intended in the beginning. As it says in Ephesians:

> But when anything is exposed by the light, it becomes visible, for anything that becomes visible is light. Therefore it says, "Awake, O sleeper, and arise from the dead, and Christ will shine on you." Look carefully then how you walk, not as unwise but as wise, making the best use of the time, because the days are evil. Therefore do not be foolish, but understand what the will of the Lord is.
>
> Eph. 5:13–17

While Jesus removes the penalty owed for sin, the effects of the fall and the consequences of sin still exist. Sin affects our relationship with God and with one another. Our sin can open the door to invite the consequences of further Satanic attack. Lastly, our sin has caused all creation to be thrown into chaos. It seems as if every couple of weeks, there's a natural disaster in the news.

Innocent children die in car crashes. People we love die from cancer. Things are not as they should be.

Finding Grace and Peace amidst Chaos

In his book *New Morning Mercies*, Paul David Tripp summarizes how the horror of the cross brought tremendous blessing. "What looked on the surface like defeat and brokenness brought us peace, forgiveness and a new beginning. . . . The hardest things in your life become the sweetest tools of grace in his wise and loving hands."[2] Tripp concludes his thought and says,

> God is at work in the lives of His children, even when we can't see it. So be careful how you make sense of your life. What looks like a disaster may, in fact, be grace. What looks like the end may be the beginning. What looks hopeless may be God's instrument to give you real and lasting hope. Your father is committed to taking what seems so bad and turning it into something that is very, very good.[3]

Of course, this doesn't mean that tragedy is good, sin is okay, or that injustice in the world should go unpunished. We can call out evil for what it is. And yet, we can also believe, in faith, that God is working in and through our disasters. And when placed in God's hands, we can trust him with our future.

Despite all the brokenness in humankind and within creation, we know God is still at work. God still creates beauty out of the chaos of our lives. As beautiful as Sedona is, the events that had to take place to create that beautiful valley might surprise you. The red-rock buttes and steep canyon walls were formed by tremendous volcanic activity under and above the earth. The volcano combined with a major flood and violent waters created the rock formations. Many of the red-rock formations look like they're stacked one on top of another. There are smooth areas up against rough, deep fractures. It's clear that thousands of years ago, something very significant happened. Geologists believe these rocks were once solid slabs that were pushed up by volcanic activity. It's strange to think that the beautiful and peaceful landscape of Sedona had such a disastrous beginning. And yet, this is a picture of how God can redeem the pressures, the fractures, brokenness, and even disasters of our own lives. Bad things—ruptures—happen. But God can still work in and through these things to create beauty. The clearest example of good coming out of brokenness is the cross of Jesus Christ.

The Apostle Paul assures us of God's love for us when we go through bad times:

Who shall separate us from the love of Christ? Shall tribulation, or distress, or persecution, or famine, or nakedness, or danger, or sword? . . . No, in all these things we are more than conquerors through him who loved us. For I am sure that neither death nor life, nor angels nor rulers, nor things present nor things to come, nor powers, nor height nor depth, nor anything else in all creation, will be able to separate us from the love of God in Christ Jesus our Lord.

Rom. 8:35; 37–39

This text is challenging and comforting at the same time. And it's a promise for you if you have ever wondered, "If God loves me, why do I have to suffer through the chaos in the world?" This text is challenging because it reminds us of our Christian ancestors being persecuted, suffering separation from families, friends, livelihoods, homes, possessions—even life itself. Yet Paul comforts them and us, assuring us that nothing can ever rip us from God's loving embrace![4] Suffering doesn't mean that God has abandoned you or that he doesn't love you or that you did something to make him angry. Whatever you are facing right now—whatever you are going through—you never have to fear the future if your faith is securely in Christ. Jesus loves you, and he encourages us in John's gospel by telling us, *"I have said these things to you, that in me you may have peace. In the world you will have tribulation. But take heart; I have overcome the world"* (John 16:33).

2

WHAT DOES THE BIBLE SAY ABOUT ALCOHOL?

"All things are lawful," but not all things are helpful. "All things are lawful," but not all things build up. Let no one seek his own good, but the good of his neighbor. Eat whatever is sold in the meat market without raising any question on the ground of conscience. For "the earth is the Lord's, and the fullness thereof." If one of the unbelievers invites you to dinner and you are disposed to go, eat whatever is set before you without raising any question on the ground of conscience. But if someone says to you, "This has been offered in sacrifice," then do not eat it, for the sake of the one who informed you, and for the sake of conscience—I do not mean your conscience, but his. For why should my liberty be determined by someone else's conscience? If I partake with thankfulness, why am I denounced because of that for which I give thanks? So, whether you eat or drink,

or whatever you do, do all to the glory of God. Give no offense to Jews or to Greeks or to the church of God, just as I try to please everyone in everything I do, not seeking my own advantage, but that of many, that they may be saved. . . . Be imitators of me, as I am of Christ.

1 Cor. 10:23–33, 11:1

Drinking alcohol was acceptable in our home when I was growing up. Like many other families, there were those who drank responsibly and those who abused it. Unfortunately, for those who abused it, alcohol was one of the contributing factors that led to physical and mental abuse, abandonment, financial hardship, crime, prison, and divorce. But that did not deter me from abusing alcohol myself.

My first experience with drinking alcohol was at the age of 15. I stole a bottle of vodka out of the liquor cabinet and headed over to my best friend's house. We mixed vodka with fruit juice and succeeded at drinking the entire bottle. The rule in my house was to be home before the street lights came on, but I didn't make it back home on time. It wasn't too long before my mom formed a search party to go find me. Mom found me up the street completely inebriated. Safely at home, the effects of my drinking began to surface. I got violently sick, and the next morning I experienced the worst hangover. This one event had such an effect on me that for years I couldn't even smell the juice we used that day without feeling sick to my stomach. From that day on, I never wanted to put anything in my body that would make me feel like that again.

At the age of 19, I was introduced to another substance. For six long years, I chose methamphetamine over every other relationship in my life. Sadly, my addiction contributed to the physical and mental abuse of myself and others. I abandoned every meaningful relationship that I had and invested every last dollar to buy more drugs. This led me to crime, jail, and divorce. So from an early age, up until my mid-20s, alcohol and drug abuse wreaked havoc in my life and the lives of others. After serving time in jail for grand theft, I quit using meth, thinking that was the source of my problems while I continued to drink alcohol on occasion.

There is much debate in Christian culture about the consumption of alcohol. Some churches are very conservative, and they oppose drinking alcohol in any quantity. Their reasoning is that they believe alcohol is inherently sinful in itself. On the flip side of that coin, there are Christians who passionately teach against legalism. They say we Christians have license in these areas, and we can do whatever we want. Addiction was the prominent issue that had dominated the lives of the people in the church where I was saved. Without any biblical conviction, abstinence made sense considering there were so many people in the church who were recovering addicts. Given my own experiences combined with the culture of this church, I latched onto the abstinence-only belief. It wasn't until I was asked by a pastor and friend to support my anti-alcohol position from the Bible that I realized I had a lot to learn. My views were inconsistent with all that the Bible had to say on the subject.

During this discovery, by God's grace, the Holy Spirit convicted me of my self-righteousness and condemning attitude. I believed the lie that alcohol and things like it were the source of the problem and that abstinence was the answer. This is a dangerous lie to believe because it minimizes the effects and consequences of sin into something we can manage. This lie also fools us into believing that we can save ourselves. Who needs a Savior from the sin of alcoholism when we can save ourselves through abstinence? My self-righteousness then fueled a prideful, divisive, judgmental, and condemning attitude toward alcohol and those who consumed it.

God began to reveal to me that the source of our problems is not outside of us (like the alcohol), but rather inside of us (our hearts). Jesus tells us,

> *There is nothing outside a person that by going into him can defile him. . . . For from within, out of the heart of man, come evil thoughts, sexual immorality, theft, murder, adultery, coveting, wickedness, deceit, sensuality, envy, slander, pride, foolishness. All these evil things come from within, and they defile a person.*
>
> Mark 7:15, 21–23

Jesus tells us here that the source of all sin comes from a heart that is corrupted by sin. God revealed to me the depth of my sin and my need for Jesus Christ to do for me what I could not do for myself. I desperately needed a new heart washed clean by the Savior's blood and the Holy Spirit's empowering to live more like Christ. God has given me opportunities to confess my sin to many that I have hurt and falsely condemned and, by God's grace, we are still friends to this day. Maybe you can relate to my story. Or maybe you have other reasons why you think alcohol isn't redeemable. Or maybe you're in control of your alcohol consumption and you don't know what the big deal is. Wherever you stand on the subject, I want to challenge you to support your position, or develop one, from the Bible.

Jesus the Drunkard?

As I began to study what the Bible says about alcohol, I found some big inconsistencies between what I had thought and what Jesus seemed to think about the subject. I had to ask myself questions such as these: If alcohol is inherently sinful, why did Jesus condone drinking? In the Gospels, Jesus was seen eating and drinking so often that he was accused by the legalistic Pharisees of being a glutton and a drunk. Jesus says in his own words, *"The Son of Man came eating and drinking, and they say, 'Look at him! A glutton and a drunkard, a friend of tax collectors and sinners!'"* (Matt. 11:19). In addition to that, Jesus's first miracle was turning water into wine, and not just any wine, but *"good wine"* (John 2:10). Top shelf wine, which was brought out only for the rarest occasions. Jesus even uses wine at the last supper to introduce the new covenant and sacrament of communion to us.

As I carefully read the Bible and reconsidered my views on alcohol, I came to a few conclusions: One, Jesus never sinned, and two, he consumed wine. I also knew that Jesus would never condone, enable, or give permission for others to sin with alcohol; that in itself would be a sin. So there had to be another explanation. But there is still tension that exists around alcohol because so many problems in our world are fueled by it. So what does the Bible say about alcohol?

To help us get to the answer, we will borrow the Apostle Paul's thinking found in 1 Corinthians. Here are some key questions that Paul gives us. Is it lawful? Is it helpful? Is it hurtful? Is it dominating? I believe these four questions will help us navigate through this very important question.

Is Drinking Alcohol Lawful?

We Christians have God's law in the Bible and the laws that govern our land as Americans. Our culture is different now, but many of the parameters still apply. First, we will start with God's law and ask this question: Is it lawful to consume alcohol? The answer is yes and no. God has not prohibited everyone from drinking alcohol, but there were circumstances in which he commanded people not to drink. In Leviticus 10 and Ezekiel 44, we are told no priests were to drink alcohol while performing their duties. What I get from this for our context is that we're not to drink on the job. It would be helpful if I wasn't drunk while I'm doing my job preaching! It was, however, lawful for a priest to consume alcohol while not working (Num. 18:12, 27, 30). In Proverbs 31:4–5, we are told no king was to drink while he was judging the law. In Esther 1, we see a bad example of a king getting drunk and making laws. God also prohibits drunkenness. In Ephesians 5, Paul writes, *"And do not get drunk with wine, for that is debauchery, but be filled with the Spirit"* (Eph. 5:18). We will discuss this verse later in this chapter.

Second, Christians are called to obey the laws of our land (Rom. 13). There are laws in America that prohibit underage drinking, drinking and driving, and public intoxication, and there are rules that prohibit employees from drinking on the job, and so on. We have God's law and man's law. So the answer to the question "Is it lawful to consume alcohol?" is both yes and no, depending on the circumstances. This is one way we can navigate through this question.

Is It Helpful?

This is a question that can get sticky. But there are some scriptures that discuss alcohol in positive terms. The Apostle Paul told Timothy to *"No longer drink only water, but use a little wine for the sake of your stomach and your frequent ailments"* (1 Tim. 5:23). Today, we can argue that we have doctors and pharmaceuticals to help with these kinds of stomach ailments. But this helps us understand that at one time, drinking alcohol was helpful in certain situations. If there had been a prohibition by God from drinking alcohol, Paul never would have given permission to Timothy to drink it.

Ecclesiastes instructs us to enjoy life with our loved ones. *"Go and eat your bread and drink your wine with a merry heart, for God already approved what you do"* (Eccles. 9:7). It can't be clearer than this. When we eat and drink responsibly with the ones that we love, God approves of it. Psalm 104:15 states that God gives wine *"to gladden the heart of man."* Amos 9:14 discusses drinking wine from your own vineyard as a sign of God's blessing. Sometimes, farmers had enough grapes left over to make wine, and this was a sign of God's blessing on their lives.

God has given you the right to drink, and it can be good and helpful. But let's be very clear here. For every positive verse in the Bible about alcohol, there are 20 verses where God warns us about the destructive power of alcohol. That leads us to the next question.

Is It Hurtful?

Even though alcohol is not inherently sinful, the abuse of alcohol, drunkenness, and addiction are sinful. The Bible calls wine a "mocker" and strong drink a "brawler" and says that whoever is led astray by it is not wise (Prov. 20:1). In 1 Corinthians 10:23–24, we are told that *"'All things are lawful,' but not all things are helpful. 'All things are lawful,' but not all things build up. Let no one seek his own good, but the good of his neighbor."* Paul ends his thought with this: *"So, whether you eat or drink, or whatever you do, do all to the glory of God"* (1 Cor. 10:31).

Do our liberties bring glory to God and good to others? God has given us the responsibility to conduct ourselves in a certain way—a way that does not cause others to stumble. God tells us in 1 Corinthians 8:9, *"But take care that this right of yours does not somehow become a stumbling block to the weak."* I don't know about you, but every time I see someone post pictures of their drinks on social media, the first thing in my mind is not "Oh look, so and so is at the pub sharing the gospel." I am not telling you whether you can or can't drink or where you can or can't drink. What I am asking you to do is prayerfully consider the choices you make and what those choices might communicate. Here are some examples. If you live in a home where a loved one struggles with alcohol, maybe there shouldn't be alcohol in your home. If you have a brother coming over for a visit who struggles with alcohol, maybe you shouldn't have bottles out of the cupboards. Being a follower of Christ is about being more like Christ. Jesus gave up his liberties for the sake of others, and we are called do the same. God calls us to put others before ourselves and be conscious of the fact that what we have the liberty to do can also be hurtful and a stumbling block for someone else.

Another way that drinking alcohol can be hurtful is when we drink in excess and become drunk. Ephesians 5:18 tells us, *"And do not get drunk with wine, for that is debauchery."* The definition of *debauchery* is excessive self-indulgence, something our culture has a real problem with. Here's what current statistics say about excessive self-indulgence. A study done by The National Institute on Alcohol Abuse and Alcoholism says nearly 88,000 people die from alcohol-related causes annually.[1] That makes alcohol the third leading preventable cause of death in the United States. More than 10 percent of American children live with a parent who has alcohol problems, and 1,825 college students between the ages of 18 and 24 die from alcohol-related injuries every year. Researchers estimate that 696,000 students are assaulted by another student who has been drinking every year. A total of 97,000 students between the ages of 18 and 24 report experiencing alcohol-related sexual assault or date rape each year. In 2014, alcohol-impaired driving fatalities accounted for 9,967 deaths (31 percent of overall driving fatalities). Also, in 2014, there were 72,559 liver disease deaths among individuals aged 12 and older, and 45.8 percent of those deaths involved alcohol. And the list goes on and on. Based on these facts alone, there is no doubt that alcohol can be hurtful.

The Apostle Paul takes it one step further for the Christian. Not only are we called not to get drunk, but we are also called to be filled with the Spirit: *"And do not get drunk with wine, for that is debauchery, but be filled with the Spirit"* (Eph. 5:18). Being drunk takes away our ability to be used by the Holy Spirit. If you're not in your right mind, how can God use you? To be drunk is to willingly remove ourselves from the ability to bless others. We're called to love and serve others. When we're not in control of our minds and bodies, how can we love those God has called us to serve?

Is It Dominating?

Lastly, drunkenness that goes unchecked can lead to addiction and what the Bible would call idolatry. Without a doubt, I can say consuming alcohol can be enslaving and dominating. Annually, 16.3 million adults aged 18 and over and 679,000 children aged 12 through 17 are diagnosed with an addiction to alcohol. The Apostle Paul tells us in 1 Corinthians 6:12, *"All things are lawful for me,"* but not all things are helpful. And later, in 1 Corinthians 10:23–24, Paul mentions the same theme again. This is where I think everything comes full circle.

Yes, we are free as Christians, but we are free to not only consider our own liberties, but we're also free to build up others. If I indulge in a freedom that keeps me from building others up in community, then I'm exercising my freedom wrongly. On the far end of the spectrum, when we become dominated by or addicted to alcohol, we give up healthy community, family, and friends—the very people we're called to love. But we can't love well if we're controlled or dominated by something. I have a friend who is definitely controlled by his addiction; he's been through rehab many times when he had to be monitored during detox in case he went into cardiac arrest. He's not just addicted, he's physically dependent on alcohol. There are many reasons why he's addicted, and it's tragic. But there's hope for him and for all of us.

Conclusion

When it comes to alcohol consumption, consider these questions again. If you can drink responsibly and it builds community, praise God! But also consider whether you are controlled or dominated by alcohol. If the answer is yes, the gospel can heal many of the issues that lead to addiction.

Consider that perhaps God has given us our rights and liberties for the sake of laying them down for others. There is no more genuine love than that. Our willingness to give up our rights for another is saying to that person, "I love you more than I love my own rights and liberties." This is the kind of love Christ shows us. It is sacrificial love. It is what Christ did when he gave up heaven to come to earth. Heaven was rightfully his. He was the only one who deserved heaven, and he gave it up for us so that we can have it too. Jesus tells us in John's Gospel, *"This is my commandment, that you love one another as I have loved you. Greater love has no one than this, that someone lay down his life for his friends"* (John 15:12–13). In our culture, we often look for an escape from pain and suffering, but Jesus willingly endured pain and suffering for us. While we may cope with pain and difficulty by using alcohol or other substances, Jesus didn't try to avoid his pain. Did you know that Jesus was even offered wine when he was on the cross to dull the pain, but he refused it? Christ laid down his own rights for the sake of others, and he's asking us to do the same.

For those who have problems with alcohol, there is hope. My out-of-control alcoholic friend I mentioned earlier loves Jesus. The conviction to fight his sin is there. But I see this man as I see the victim in the Good Samaritan story. God loves the guy that is dying on the side of the road. Whenever I come in contact with my friend, I am going to intentionally bind up his wounds, care for him, love him, and be willing to take him to a place where he can get extended care, and put it on my tab. Seriously. This is the kind of community we want to be, and this is the love and care that Jesus gives to us. Jesus said, *"Come to me, all who labor and are heavy laden, and I will give you rest"* (Matt. 11:28). There are far too many people burdened by guilt, shame, grief, sorrow, stress, worry, depression, fear, and hopelessness. Jesus wants us to come to him and find rest, and as it says in 1 Peter 5:7, we can cast all of our anxieties on him because he cares for us.

3

WHAT DOES THE BIBLE SAY ABOUT DINOSAURS?

As I mentioned in the introduction, our church hosted a summer preaching series addressing common questions Christians ask about the Bible and the faith. We wanted to make sure that everyone had an opportunity to ask their questions, and that included 10-year-old boys! In case you haven't heard, boys are really into dinosaurs. So a natural question coming from a boy is, "What does the Bible say about dinosaurs?" We'll address a few things in this chapter. First, we will consider whether dinosaurs are mentioned in the Bible, and second, we'll address some of the questions that may arise regarding issues of science and the potential age of the earth. Most importantly, we'll consider issues of sin, death, and salvation because they will help us explain why dinosaurs are no longer here.

The topic of dinosaurs has been debated in the church for hundreds of years, and the devil has used this topic to create division in the church. While I believe there are things worth dividing over, let me be clear, dinosaurs is not one of them. Often, these debates can veer into speculation about the age of the earth and the coexistence of man and dinosaurs. These are all great topics to argue and discuss, but they're not topics worth dividing over. When it comes to the Christian faith, there are many truths that we hold close. These truths include the authority of the Bible; the fact that Jesus lived, died, and rose again; and the belief that the miracles recorded in the Bible really happened. There are other debates like whether to baptize babies or only believers who can profess faith for themselves. Topics such as these are held a bit more open-handed, as they don't have to do with issues of a person's salvation. Likewise, questions surrounding whether dinosaurs and men walked the earth at the same time and the age of the earth are not salvation issues and are not worth Christians dividing over.

First things first: Does the Bible mention dinosaurs? I believe the answer is yes.

The word *dinosaur* doesn't appear in the Bible because the word didn't exist when the Bible was written. Dinosaur means "terrible lizard." This name was given to describe the first fossil found in the 19th century, a little over 200 years ago. The Bible teaches us that God created everything—the earth, stars, sun, moon, plants, animals, and humans. Therefore, because dinosaurs existed, God had to create them. When he created the animals, this is what God said:

> And God said, "Let the waters swarm with swarms of living creatures, and let birds fly above the earth across the expanse of the heavens." So God created the great sea creatures and every living creature that moves, with which the waters swarm, according to their kinds, and every winged bird according to its kind. And God saw that it was good. And God blessed them, saying, "Be fruitful and multiply and fill the waters in the seas, and let birds multiply on the earth." And there was evening and there was morning, the fifth day. And God said, "Let the earth bring forth living creatures according to their kinds—livestock and creeping things and beasts of the earth according to their kinds." And it was so. And God made the beasts of the earth according to their kinds and the livestock according to their kinds, and everything that creeps on the ground according to its kind. And God saw that it was good.
>
> Gen. 1:20–25

Genesis 1 is an account of God's creation, and what we read does not eliminate the possibility of dinosaurs being part of his creation. God distinguishes the livestock from every creeping things and beast of the earth. Certainly some dinosaurs would creep, and many could easily be described as a "beast." The Bible mentions dragons, sea monsters, and serpents nearly 30 times in the Old Testament; these references can easily describe what we consider dinosaur-like creatures. God gives Job a description of what very well could be a dinosaur:

> Behold, Behemoth, which I made as I made you; he eats grass like an ox. Behold, his strength in his loins, and his power in the muscles of his belly. He makes his tail stiff like a cedar; the sinews of his thighs are knit together (a sinew is tough fibrous muscle and tissue). His bones are tubes of bronze, his limbs like bars of iron. "He is the first of the works of God; let him who made him bring near his sword! For the mountains yield food for him where all the wild beasts play."
>
> Job 40:15–20

This sounds a lot like a dinosaur! We can argue that there are many animals that have great strength, but what one living creature has all these physical features? While we don't have a living example of this creature, we do have fossils. Having this creature mentioned in the book of Job convinces me that the Bible gives clear evidence of the existence of dinosaurs. More importantly, these verses strongly suggest that man and dinosaurs existed at the same time. This helps us in our belief that the Bible is literal and without error, and that leads to our next topic surrounding creation and the trustworthiness of Scripture.

Can God's Scripture Be Trusted?

Let's begin by determining whether the Bible can be trusted. Is the Bible without error? Does it accurately inform us about creation and the beginning of time? Does the Bible accurately inform us about history? Does it speak accurately into our present day, and does the Word of God speak accurately about our future? These are all great questions, and I believe the answer is yes. There is a section in our church's statement of faith that says this:

> We believe that the Bible is completely true and perfect. The Bible is the infallible Word of God and is the final authority for all matters of faith and living. As the voice of the almighty God, we believe that Scripture carries all of the authority of God himself. Therefore any tradition, man, or practice inside and outside of the church must fall under the submission of Scripture.

This is the position I take with God's Word, and that will inform my thinking on what follows in this chapter.

Before we begin, it makes sense to address again that Christians have differing points of view when it comes to issues of science and creation. One of the reasons for this is partially due to "hermeneutics." That's just a fancy word for how we read and interpret the Bible. To put it in simple terms, when we approach a book of the Bible or a particular topic from the text, we have to ask ourselves questions such as this: Who was this written for in the original context? What concerns were the writings addressing? The reason this is important is because the Bible is not intended to be a science textbook. If we approach it that way, we are in danger of adding meaning to a text it may not be intending to convey. However, when the Bible speaks about a "behemoth"—a creature that is likely a dinosaur, we can take it at face value as true. Dinosaurs existed. We know that they existed from the scientific evidence, and there is a strong argument that people and dinosaurs existed on the earth at the same time. This introduces some challenges into the discussion about the age of the earth, as I'll show below.

Is the Earth Young or Old?

The Bible reveals to us that God created all things in six days and he rested on the seventh day. There is much debate surrounding whether these were six literal, 24-hour days, or whether there were gaps between each day. Some argue that the word *epoch* (which is translated as "day" in our Bibles) is a general term for a measure of time. Some argue that perhaps each epoch was much longer than a literal 24-hour day.

Early in my faith, I adopted the belief that the earth and animals are old and humans are young. It made it easier to explain away things such as the age of dinosaurs and the coexistence of dinosaurs and man. But as my conviction of the infallibility of Scripture grew, I had to do the hard work of reasoning without contradicting Scripture. Again, I know that some Jesus-loving, Bible-believing Christians differ with me on this, and that's OK. But this is my conviction, and I think it's a reasonable one.

Over time, I realized that my belief in an old creation of the earth and animals, but a young creation of human beings was inconsistent with historical evidences outside of the Bible. What I've learned is that nearly every ancient civilization has some sort of art depicting giant dinosaur-like creatures. Archaeologists have found petroglyphs, artifacts, and even little clay figurines that resemble modern depictions of dinosaurs. Rock carvings have been found in South America, showing men riding what looks to be a triceratops. Roman mosaics, Mayan pottery, and Babylonian city walls all testify to the coexistence of dinosaurs and man. Some of the most convincing evidences are the fossilized footprints of humans found alongside dinosaur tracks.

What about the Age of Dinosaurs?

Consider for a moment taking God at his word and believing he created everything in six literal days. Here is what we are told. All the animals were created on the fourth and fifth days, and God created the first humans — Adam and Eve — on the sixth day. In Genesis 4 through 9, God gives us the genealogy of Adam and Eve's children and describes events leading up to the days of Noah. When we do the math from the time of creation to the days of Noah, the total comes to approximately 4,500 years. Then from the time of Noah, God gives us the genealogies throughout the Old Testament all the way to the New Testament, which leads us to the time of Jesus Christ. Our current calendar started after Jesus's death. Christ came to earth roughly 2,000 years ago. When we consider all these timelines, we can estimate that the earth's age is somewhere around 6,000 to 7,000 years old. This contradicts the old earth creationists' and evolutionists' theory that the earth is 45 million years old.

Just recently, I read an article on the Institute for Creation Research website (www.icr.org) stating that dinosaur fossils have been found with traces of soft tissue-like cartilage and marrow on the bones. This was a huge discovery and great victory for young earth creationists who believe the Bible is true and accurate regarding timelines, because soft tissue would decompose over millions of years. So, if we are to believe that dinosaurs and humans were created in the same week and coexisted, the next logical question is, What happened to the dinosaurs?

What Happened to the Dinosaurs?

The Bible tells us that in the days of Noah, God looked down and saw that man was absolutely corrupted by sin. God expressed himself as being deeply sorry he ever created man. As an act of mercy, God chose to judge the earth with a flood. Accordingly, he wiped out a whole generation of people along with the animals. The only exception to this judgment was Noah, his family, and two of every kind of animal. God gave Noah grace and called him to build an ark. When he was finished building the ark, two of every kind of animal were led into the ark. God then closed the door and flooded the earth. The Bible explains that everyone and everything on the earth were swallowed up in this watery grave. Humans and every kind of animal—including dinosaurs—drowned and were covered in tons of mud as the waters covered the land. Because of this quick burial, many of the animals would have died intact, which explains the fossils found in the ground today. (In Chapter 8, I answer the question Why did God flood the earth?)

Some argue that the size of the ark was not large enough to carry a dinosaur. But God could have sent young dinosaurs with Noah. We are not told. After the flood, the new world would have been much different. Considering everything on the earth was dead, the competition for food and survival must have been even greater. Maybe this competition for food caused large dinosaurs to eventually die out and become extinct. What we do have today are smaller beasts like rhinoceroses and smaller reptiles like crocodiles and alligators, all of which resemble dinosaurs.

We all can agree that dinosaurs existed for a time, but now they are extinct. The way a species becomes extinct is through death, and the Bible tells us that death exists because of sin. Unfortunately, everything sin touches dies. This points back to Genesis 3 when sin and death entered into human history, and death spread through all the earth and to every living creature. Every time we see the bones of dinosaurs, we should consider more pressing issues like sin, death, judgment, and the good news about salvation and new life through Jesus Christ. To address this, God spoke to us through the Apostle Paul in Romans 5. He says:

Therefore, just as sin came into the world through one man, and death through sin, and so death spread to all men because all sinned. . . . But the free gift is not like the trespass. For if many died through one man's trespass, much more have the grace of God and the free gift by the grace of that one man Jesus Christ abounded for many. And the free gift is not like the result of that one man's sin. . . . For if, because of one man's trespass, death reigned through that one man, much more will those who receive the abundance of grace and the free gift of righteousness reign in life through the one man Jesus Christ.

Rom. 5:12, 15, 17

Conclusion

To recap, based on an inquisitive boy's question, we considered whether dinosaurs are mentioned in the Bible. I'm pretty confident the answer to that question is yes. This dinosaur research led us to other questions about creation, questions that are important but debatable. While there seems to be conflict between popular science and what the Bible says at face value, the more important issues to consider are issues of life, sin, death, judgment, and the good news about salvation and new life through Jesus Christ. The debates will rage on, and Christians will continue to disagree on these issues. What we shouldn't debate about are the more important truths surrounding sin, death, and salvation.

There is good news for us. Paul would tell us, *"For the wages of sin is death, but the gift of God is eternal life in Christ Jesus our Lord"* (Rom. 6:23). Everything sin touches dies, including our Lord Jesus Christ. Our perfect sinless Savior took all of our sin upon himself, and he died so we don't have to. Then he took our sins to the grave. Paul writes in 2 Corinthians 5:21, *"For our sake he made him to be sin who knew no sin, so that in him we might become the righteousness of God."* Jesus paid our debt, taking our sins to the grave and, on the third day, Jesus rose from that grave. Jesus is alive, and he has conquered death for our sake! Anyone who believes in him will be saved. God adopts us as his children and promises us life everlasting. Jesus will soon return, and he promises to judge the earth again, cleansing the earth of all sin. Listen to what he tells us in Revelation. *"He will wipe away every tear from our eyes, and death shall be no more, neither shall there be mourning, nor crying, nor pain anymore, for the former things have passed away"* (Rev. 21:4).

Ultimately, dinosaurs are a testimony of God's unlimited creativity. The fact that they do not exist anymore points to the sin that ushered in death, which led to the extinction of dinosaurs. The fall and death both point to our need for a Savior. It is beyond our capability to save ourselves or this world. But we have a wonderful king in Jesus who is able. The life that we long for will never be completely satisfied until we are in Jesus's kingdom. I pray that we would hold fast to the promise of Jesus's return when he will set everything straight and establish his kingdom here on earth. My hope is that in Christ's new kingdom, dinosaurs will exist! I want to see them and experience what God wanted us to see and experience when he created the earth.

4

WHAT DOES THE BIBLE SAY ABOUT DIVORCE?

Years before I became the pastor of Encounter Church, I was an associate pastor in a church that underwent quite a bit of turmoil. As a result, Sheila and I—as well as several others in our church—decided it was time to leave. Pastor Jeff Ludington was a friend who knew of our situation; so he asked if Sheila and I would like to visit his church. We took him up on the invitation, we loved it, and eventually we became members. Over time, Pastor Jeff asked me if I would consider being an elder with the goal of pastoral ministry. After much prayer, I agreed to accept.

Agreeing to this role meant that I was under the leadership of Pastor Jeff, and he insisted that I wouldn't preach until I'd gone through a period of discipleship and continued theological education. He made it clear I wouldn't be preaching until he said I was ready, and I agreed to his terms. Secretly and pridefully, I thought to myself, "As soon as this guy hears me preach, I'll be up on stage on a regular basis!" It was a three-year process of personal growth and learning before I finally got my opportunity to preach. I can't remember exactly what I preached, but what I do remember was that, later that evening, my email inbox filled up with some encouraging comments that were overshadowed by more than 25 negative critiques of my sermon. Many of these emails came from people who were respected members of our church. I was devastated.

Later the next week, I went into Pastor Jeff's office feeling discouraged. I told him about all the negative feedback I'd received and that I felt it was a sign that I needed to be done with my pursuit of eldership and pastoral ministry. Pastor Jeff was baffled and even angry. In response he said, "Who gives these people the right to speak in a way that will make you change the direction of your life?" I didn't have a good answer, but I began to realize I was being controlled by other people's opinion of me.

What I learned that day was that it's not wise to let just anyone influence me. Pastor Jeff taught me that day that I need to give the permission for people to speak authoritatively into my life. The people who qualify must—without a doubt—love and respect me and want the best for me. Of course, the main authority in my life is Jesus, his Word, and God's calling upon my life. I would also listen to my wife, my pastors, and my elders. I know that they want the best for me. They pray for me regularly, they love me, and they're not afraid to have hard conversations with me. I know that their hearts are not to destroy me, but to restore me and see me grow.

You may be asking what any of this has to do with the subject of divorce. But I do have a point in telling this story. The point is, all too often, we give the wrong people weight and authority in our lives. My call to pastoral leadership was and is a sacred thing. Marriage is also sacred. But all too often, we allow the opinions of others to change the course of our lives. We often listen to the surrounding culture or unwise "friends" as our counselors. God wants better for us.

When it comes to the subject of marriage, let's prayerfully consider who or what we will allow to inform our thoughts and opinions. In this chapter, we'll discuss why God would allow for biblical divorce. But please hear this: Jesus died for every sin, even the one that threatens your marriage. God gives every believer the gifts of grace, forgiveness, confession, repentance, reconciliation, and restoration. But not all of God's people operate this way, and not all of God's people marry believers. So God in his mercy has allowed divorce—but only under the most extreme cases.

Is It Better to Not Marry?

There is a general fear of marriage in our culture. Our culture seems to say, maybe it's better to not get married at all, and this conclusion makes sense when you look at the statistics. According to the U.S. Centers for Disease Control (CDC), which are in charge of the National Center for Health Statistics, approximately 50 percent of all marriages end in divorce. Two-thirds of all second marriages fail, and 75 percent of third marriages also end in divorce.[1] Sadly, the divorce rate among Christians is nearly identical to the divorce rate of nonbelievers. And yet, Jesus tells us that divorce was never God's plan for marriage. Instead, he says that God's intention for marriage is oneness. The two shall become one flesh, and what God has joined together, let no man separate. I'm certain that no couple gets married thinking that they would ever get a divorce. But marriage involves two sinful people, and God knows this. That is why he sent Jesus.

Did Jesus Allow Divorce?

Whenever we read the Bible, it's important to ask why Jesus said the things he did. We can figure this out when we consider who Jesus was talking to and the issue he was addressing in the moment. When Jesus spoke about sexual immorality and divorce, he was speaking to the religious leaders of his day. Jesus was drilling down into the heart of the religious leaders who were issuing certificates of divorce that allowed men to leave their wives for literally any reason. Much like our culture today, this resulted in broken homes and the abandonment of many women and children. So, in an attempt to rebuke these religious leaders, Jesus responded by saying,

Have you not read that he who created them from the beginning made them male and female, and said, "Therefore a man shall leave his father and his mother and hold fast to his wife, and the two shall become one

flesh?" So they are no longer two but one flesh. What therefore God has joined together, let not man separate.

Matt. 19:4–6

The religious leaders with whom Jesus was talking should have been familiar with God's intent for marriage and the purpose of divorce. This is why, before Jesus gives them an answer to their question, he asks, *"have you not read?"* as if to say, you should know better! But like many of us, when their lifestyle and actions were challenged, they looked to justify what they were doing by using Moses as an example. Jesus quickly corrects them by saying, *"Because of your hardness of heart Moses allowed you to divorce your wives, but from the beginning it was not so. And I say to you: whoever divorces his wife, except for sexual immorality, and marries another, commits adultery"* (Matt. 19:8–9).

Jesus shifts the blame of Moses and points it back to them. Their hearts were hardened to the truth of God's Word and his intent for marriage and divorce. The religious leaders were issuing these certificates without cause, which essentially gave permission for these men to commit adultery against their spouses. The most merciful thing Moses could do because of the hardness of their hearts was issue a certificate of divorce and release the other spouse to remarry after being abandoned. So you can see how having a proper understanding of the context when interpreting Scripture is so important when making decisions.

Jesus corrects the religious leaders and instructs them that they are not supposed to issue divorce certificates, except for sexual immorality. But this needs some explanation, too. The Greek word Jesus uses for sexual immorality is *porneia*. This is where we get our word for pornography. Porneia can mean any form of sexual sin. You can see how easy it was for the religious leaders to justify issuing certificates of divorce, as for all practical purposes, misinterpreting Jesus here meant everyone had a valid reason to divorce. If we're honest, everyone has sinned sexually in some way against God and their spouse. Sexual immorality can range from having an impure thought to the act of adultery. So again, it is vitally important to interpret these scriptures with the audience in mind.

Had Jesus been counseling a couple that was struggling through sexual immorality, I don't believe he'd issue a certificate of divorce as quickly as the religious leaders were guilty of doing. I believe Jesus's first step would be to extend grace to the couple, forgive their sins, and encourage them to confess their sins to one another. His next step would be to encourage repentance, forgiveness, obedience, and reconciliation. Jesus would want this couple to experience more than mercy brought through divorce; he would want them to have the fullness of God's grace by which salvation, transformation, restoration, and redemption could be manifested in their marriage.

You may recall that I said this before: everything sin touches dies. If sin in our marriages goes unaddressed, then it can result in the death of our marriages. But the good news is that Jesus willingly took the sin that threatens to kill our marriages to the cross. He died to forgive us of all sins—including sexual immorality. He rose from the grave in victory over death. Jesus is alive, and he has conquered death for our sake! The good news of Jesus's life and death not only reconciles us to God, but it also has the power to reconcile us to one another. Reconciliation is not easy, and the guilty party never deserves it, but that's how grace works. When we wonder how to handle the sin that leads to devastating problems in our marriages, we should humbly look at how God handled our sin that was leading us to our death. Jesus has forgiven us and given us a new life, and his mercies are new every morning.

The book of Hosea describes God's people—the nation of Israel—as an unfaithful wife who was continually unfaithful to the covenant relationship she had with the Lord. Even though Israel deserved to be divorced and abandoned, God pursued his wandering bride relentlessly and drew her back to himself. Jesus is described as the great bridegroom who faithfully pursued his people at great cost to himself. Reconciliation wasn't easy. It cost him his life.

While divorce is permissible in some circumstances, reconciliation should always be the goal. Divorce might be the only solution, but it should always be the last option, a decision that you should never make on your own. Seek the counsel of a qualified Christian counselor or your pastor and elders—people who love you and want the best for you. Let them help you navigate through this season of life. Have the courage to allow them to walk with you and exhaust every possible hope of restoration for your marriage. And be a person of faith. Have faith in Jesus who has the power to save, transform, restore, and redeem your marriage.

Divorce and Remarriage Are God's Grace and Mercy for the Abandoned

Other than infidelity, there is only one other instance in the Bible where God gives pastors and counselors clear permission to suggest divorce. It is in the case of an unbelieving spouse who abandons a believing spouse. Here's what the Apostle Paul says on the subject:

> To the married I give this charge (not I, but the Lord): the wife should not separate from her husband (but if she does, she should remain unmarried or else be reconciled to her husband), and the husband should not divorce his wife. To the rest I say (I, not the Lord) that if any brother has a wife who is an unbeliever, and she consents to live with him, he should not divorce her. If any woman has a husband who is an unbeliever, and he consents to live with her, she should not divorce him. For the unbelieving husband is made holy because of his wife, and the unbelieving wife is made holy because of her husband. Otherwise your children would be unclean, but as it is, they are holy. But if the unbelieving partner separates, let it be so. In such cases the brother or sister is not enslaved. God has called you to peace. For how do you know, wife, whether you will save your husband? Or how do you know, husband, whether you will save your wife?
>
> 1 Cor. 7:10–16

First and most importantly, Paul is leaning heavily on the side of saving and restoring the marriage in these verses. He, too, is exhausting every means for the salvation of unbelieving spouses and reconciliation of their marriages. The only exception comes in verse 15 where Paul says that, in the case of a believer married to an unbeliever, if the unbeliever leaves and abandons the relationship, the believer is not under any obligation to stay in the marriage. Rather, "God has called us to peace." I've counseled many people—mostly women—who have been abandoned by their spouses for any number of reasons. The trauma of abandonment combined with the guilt and shame that Satan sows into their hearts and minds is devastating. Couples do not marry expecting that either of them will be left abandoned and alone. But I have seen far too many people abandoned who are left alone and lonely, broken, and hopeless. In many cases, they are abandoned and forced to support themselves and their kids alone. This experience leaves people hurt, hopeless, and fearful of ever trusting another person again. If you have been abandoned by your spouse, then hear the love and the grace of God: *"But if the unbelieving partner separates, let it be so. In such cases the brother or sister is not enslaved. God has called you to peace"* (1 Cor. 7:15).

You no longer have to be weighed down by the failure of a spouse who abandoned you. You no longer have to be tormented by Satan's guilt trips. You no longer have to be enslaved by the fear of never having a godly spouse. God knows that it is not good for you to be alone and, according to Genesis 2, he will make a spouse suitable for you. Let the grace of God bring peace to your mind. He wants to free you from the guilt and shame, heal your heart, and restore your life. Embrace the promise in Joel 2:35 where God says that he *"will restore to you the years that the swarming locust has eaten."*

Is There Any Other Exception for Divorce?

The Bible does not give any clear grounds for divorce other than the two instances we've covered (sexual immorality and abandonment). But that doesn't mean there are no other reasons God would allow divorce. While it is never wise to presume upon God's Word or to think we know the heart of God on every matter, I cannot imagine it would be God's desire for you to remain with an abusive spouse or a spouse that forces you to engage in criminal activity, or the like. Even though the Bible isn't clear in these instances, we have to believe that God is a good father who wants to protect his children from evil. In such a case, get the authorities involved, or call the police if you need to. Separate yourself and your children immediately, and get somewhere safe. Safety for you and your children is of first importance. Then seek the counsel of a qualified Christian counselor, pastor, or elders to help you navigate through this season of your life.

Is There Hope If I Have Divorced My Spouse for the Wrong Reasons?

For those that have divorced a spouse without biblical grounds, I want you to know that divorce is not an unforgivable sin. Jesus died for all of your sins and, if you have placed your faith in him, you are forgiven. Perhaps God would call you to respond in faith to the grace that you have been given and reconcile with your former spouse. At a minimum, God would call you to confess your sins, repent, and make peace with your former spouse. Sometimes, this is all you can do. Or perhaps God wants full reconciliation and restoration of your marriage. Again, it's best to navigate these waters with a trusted advisor who will love you and guide you to make the best decisions.

What Can I Do to Divorce-Proof My Marriage?

I still joke with Sheila, saying God must have blinded her when she met me because I will never understand what she saw in me. By God's amazing grace, on April 26, 2003, he gave me the greatest gift in the world. He gave me his daughter, and Sheila became my wife. He is also giving us the grace and faith necessary not only to survive but to thrive. As the old saying goes, marriages that are made in heaven need to be maintained on earth. I asked Sheila to help me with this section of the book because we did not want to end without giving you some tools to help enrich your marriage. With all of the sobering statistics about divorce, we hope and pray that these principles will bless, enrich, and strengthen your marriage.

Be United

The first thing a couple can do is be united in their beliefs. The Apostle Paul instructs us, *"Do not be unequally yoked with unbelievers. For what partnership has righteousness with lawlessness? Or what fellowship has light with darkness?"* (2 Cor. 6:14).

A yoke is normally used in farming. It is put around an animal's neck to control the direction and speed of the animal as it travels around the farm. Sometimes yokes are made for two animals to pull heavy loads. Now imagine this: If you are a horse yoked to a cow, you're going to get frustrated since each animal will consistently be moving in opposing directions! The horse is naturally drawn to the stables, while the cow is naturally drawn to the fields. In the same way, believers and unbelievers have different operating principles and directions in life. So, it is important to be united in your beliefs, your faith, and your convictions.

If you are already in a marriage with an unbeliever, you have the responsibility to not compromise your beliefs and stay with that person. Being Christlike to an unbelieving spouse is one way that your spouse can come to know Christ. Jesus loves your unbelieving spouse with an everlasting love, and he wants to forgive them of their sin and call them to a new life in Christ. Jesus is the most loving gift you can give to your spouse, and it is the only gift that will last forever. This leads us to the next thing you can do to bless and enrich your marriage: be loving.

Be Loving

Our spouses need to be loved like Christ loves us. The Apostle Paul gives us an example of Christ's love which is the truest definition of what love is:

> If I speak in the tongues of men and of angels, but have not love, I am a noisy gong or a clanging cymbal. And if I have prophetic powers, and understand all mysteries and all knowledge, and if I have all faith, so as to remove mountains, but have not love, I am

nothing. If I give away all I have, and if I deliver up my body to be burned, but have not love, I gain nothing. Love is patient and kind; love does not envy or boast; it is not arrogant or rude. It does not insist on its own way; it is not irritable or resentful; it does not rejoice at wrongdoing, but rejoices with the truth. Love bears all things, believes all things, hopes all things, endures all things. Love never ends. As for prophecies, they will pass away; as for tongues, they will cease; as for knowledge, it will pass away. For we know in part and we prophesy in part, but when the perfect comes, the partial will pass away. When I was a child, I spoke like a child, I thought like a child, I reasoned like a child. When I became a man, I gave up childish ways. For now we see in a mirror dimly, but then face to face. Now I know in part; then I shall know fully, even as I have been fully known. So now faith, hope, and love abide, these three; but the greatest of these is love.

1 Cor. 13

Early in our marriage, Sheila and I were fortunate to attend a conference with Dr. Gary Chapman, the author of *The Five Love Languages*. He teaches that there are five primary love languages: words of affirmation, quality time, receiving gifts, acts of service, and physical touch.[2] Dr. Chapman taught us that our primary love language is typically not the same as our spouse. This is a challenge because we typically love others the way we like to be loved. My primary love language is words of affirmation. What I discovered is that I was speaking my love language to Sheila, leaving her feeling unloved. Sheila's primary love language is acts of service. Who would have thought that vacuuming the carpet, fixing the faucet, and helping her run errands would be an expression of love toward my wife? But it is! Learning one another's love language will be one of the most important things you ever learn. It taught me that my laziness and broken commitments made more work for Sheila, communicating to her that her feelings don't matter. Ultimately, my goal is to love Sheila like Christ, who said, *"For even the Son of Man came not to be served but to serve"* (Mark 10:45). I truly want to love her like Jesus, but I know I am not Jesus. This leads us to the next thing you can do to bless and enrich your marriage: be forgiving.

Be Forgiving

The Apostle Paul reminds us to practice kindness, love, patience, and forgiveness toward each another. Here's what he says:

> *Put on then, as God's chosen ones, holy and beloved, compassionate hearts, kindness, humility, meekness, and patience, bearing with one another and, if one has a complaint against another, forgiving each other; as the Lord has forgiven you, so you also must forgive. And above all these put on love, which binds everything together in perfect harmony.*
>
> Col. 3:12–14

We are going to make mistakes along the way. We need to trust in the grace of God and forgive one another. Some of the most important words we can say are, "I am sorry," and "I forgive you." When we feel the pain of sin, sorrow leads to repentance—first with God, and then with one another. Not only do forgiveness and repentance strengthen a marriage, but they also encourage us to admit our faults. If you're always walking on eggshells because you can't make a mistake in your marriage, then there's a huge problem. Your marriage needs to be a safe place to make mistakes. When the marriage relationship is a safe place to fail, it opens the door for God to work humility, confession, forgiveness, repentance, reconciliation, and restoration in the life of your marriage. By God's grace, this is the way our marriages can not only survive, but thrive! Most strong marriages are strong because the couples have worked through and climbed out of some of the deepest valleys.

Be in Prayer

Couples who pray together stay together. Prayer takes your marriage to God and brings God into your marriage. In the Gospel of John, Jesus gives us an illustration of how we are to be connected to him through prayer. He says:

> I am the vine; you are the branches. Whoever abides in me and I in him, he it is that bears much fruit, for apart from me you can do nothing. If anyone does not abide in me he is thrown away like a branch and withers; and the branches are gathered, thrown into the fire, and burned. If you abide in me, and my words abide in you, ask whatever you wish, and it will be done for you.
>
> John 15:5–7

Prayer is how we stay connected to Jesus. As a couple, pray together and pray often. Declare your need for Jesus in your marriage. Confess the sins that have threatened your marriage, and thank God for the forgiveness that comes to us from Jesus. Pray for the gift of repentance and the power of the Spirit to work reconciliation into your marriage. Pray for everything that touches your marriage: your kids, your family, your work, your church, and the like.

Be in His Word

If our marriages are going to produce the type of fruit that Jesus is illustrating in this next verse, then we have to be connected to him and his Word. *"If you abide in my word, you are truly my disciples, and you will know the truth, and the truth will set you free"* (John 8:31–32).

If you really want to change any area of your life, then you need to know and apply the truth in that area. If you want to change your finances, you've got to know what God said about finances, and apply that truth to your life. If you want to change your marriage, you've got to know what God has said about marriage, and apply that truth to your life. God's Word is the truth, but the truth is more that a set of principles or guidelines to live by because truth is a person. Jesus said, *"I am the way, and the truth, and the life"* (John 14:6).

And because Jesus is the truth, then you can trust what he says. The alternative is to rely upon the voices of the world, whose advice is limited at best, and comes out of brokenness and hurt relationships at worst. The worst advice typically comes out of a survival mindset and is not rooted in an understanding of Scripture. Jesus's words are true; you can trust them for your marriage, and they bring life, hope, compassion, forgiveness, power, and transformation into relationships.

We Need Faith

Our culture often paints a fairy-tale picture of marriage and when real life doesn't match the fairy tale, people want to bail out. Marriage is hard, and there's suffering attached because marriage means that there are two sinners coming together. James writes,

Count it all joy, my brothers, when you meet trials of various kinds, for you know that the testing of your faith produces steadfastness. And let steadfastness have its full effect, that you may be perfect and complete, lacking in nothing.

James 1:2–4

We're all going to make mistakes, and sometimes our mistakes are huge. Things happen that will sometimes be out of our control. But this brokenness doesn't have to be the last word. There is hope because God promises to be faithful, and he will see us through every circumstance that we face in this life.

One of the roughest seasons in our marriage was when we received the devastating news of the untimely death of Sheila's brother. Eric was an awesome, fun-loving man who tragically lost his life at the young age of 41. This rocked us, and our marriage was tested like never before. Thankfully, we did not have to go through this alone. We had our faith in Jesus, and we had our friends—who still to this day are committed to loving, praying, serving, counseling, and sometimes just plain being there for us when times get tough. I wanted to fix this situation, but it was out of my control. Nothing was going to stop the hurt inside my wife's heart. There were times when I sat silently in prayer while holding my wife as she wept for hours. Faith in Jesus, a strong shoulder, and thousands of desperate prayers were all I had to offer my wife.

Thankfully, Eric's faith was securely in Jesus Christ. This means Eric's death had no victory over his life, and he lives on in heaven with Jesus now. It is with confidence that Eric, being a believer in Jesus Christ, heard our Lord say, "Well done good and faithful servant. Now enter into my rest" (Matt. 25:21). We know it was nothing that he had done to earn such an honor, but only through faith in knowing that Christ lived that faithful life on his behalf. I long to hear those words myself, one day, and everyone who has faith in Jesus Christ longs for that day as well.

While it is a thrill to know the faithful are set free, my wife and I, along with our family, are still struck with deep and sincere grief. But we will see Eric again in God's kingdom. That is the Good News that we will continue to remind ourselves of until peace and comfort consume our hearts. Honestly, I don't think that's completely possible this side of heaven, but we will hold on to the hope that comes with our faith. We know peace and comfort will come even if it means that we have to wait to enter into the eternal peace and comfort that awaits us—and every believer—in God's kingdom. That's where Eric is, and that's where we will see him again.

Sheila and I pray that you never have to experience such tragedy, but when marriage gets tough, God wants us to remain faithful—first in him, and second with one another. It is in the trying times that he does his best work in us. Although God is not the cause of our problems, he will use them to strengthen our faith in him for our marriages. We are believers after all! Let us believe in the atoning work of the cross and believe that God can restore all things. We must believe that God can heal, redeem, and restore every broken piece in our lives.

5

WHAT DOES THE BIBLE SAY ABOUT HOMOSEXUALITY?

When I became the lead pastor of Encounter Christian Church in April 2014, one of my goals was to meet with everyone serving in ministry. Michael was a man who was excited about serving at the church. As with all of the leaders with whom I scheduled appointments, Michael and I met over lunch. My goal was to get to know him personally, ask Michael about his relationship with Jesus, and cast vision with him for ministry.

Michael shared that he started coming to our church with his parents over 20 years ago. He served in the youth ministry where he found great joy in teaching our youth the Bible. The conversation shifted to me asking about his relationship with Jesus. Michael said it was really good with the exception of one incident that really challenged his faith. He then explained how he had been hurt by a very prominent leader in the church who thought he should not be serving in ministry. I was sensing I knew the reason, and God gave me the courage to ask Michael if it was all right if we address "the elephant in the room," to which he nervously replied, "OK." I then asked him if this incident had anything to do with him being gay. Later, Michael told me that in that moment, it was like he could feel the air being sucked out of the room. He was hesitant to answer my question because he knew that once the truth came out, he would not be able to take the words back. Maybe I would treat him like that other leader or even worse, ostracize him altogether. Thankfully, God gave Michael the courage to answer, and he replied, "Yes, this all happened because she found out I am gay." I simply didn't know what to say next. I was just so thankful that Michael trusted me with such a personal part of his life. By God's grace, he continued to share his story.

Growing up, Michael felt "different" from an early age. He had dated a few girls in his teens and twenties, and when things began to get physical, he automatically knew there was no real attraction to the opposite sex. There was simply no denying the way he felt. Michael's dad was a local sergeant in the Sheriff's Department; his mom worked in the school district, and they were all part of our church. He knew from the Bible that to act out on his feelings was a sin. Michael heard all of the horrible anti-gay messages like, "God hates gays," "faggots are going to hell," and "homosexuality is an abomination." These messages left him understandably afraid to be known. So he did his best to repress his feelings in fear of bringing shame on his family and being ostracized from the church.

I didn't understand what it was like to struggle with same-sex attraction, and I wanted to know. Michael then asked me something that blew me away. He asked me if I remembered my first heartbreak. I immediately knew the answer to his question. "Yes, I was 13 years old when I had my first crush and heartbreak in the summer of 1985 with the girl next door." Then Michael said, "No, not a crush. I mean some serious heartbreak." I was held captive by the seriousness of his correction. He continued to testify that when he was in his 20s, he had his first relationship with a man. For the first time, his attraction to the same sex was what he felt he had been missing all along. He was finally in the relationship that felt right. At the same time, he was feeling the conviction that what he was doing was wrong. Torn between the relationship with this man and his faith in Jesus, Michael chose to break off the relationship. He then explained to me the heartbreak that he felt after making this decision. He said this led him to a point of depression that can only be compared to the sense of suffering and loss caused by the death of a loved one. Admittedly, I was taken back. I did not understand same-sex attraction, but I understood the heartbreak and deep loss that Michael had experienced. I suddenly realized I was no different than Michael. The only difference was the sex of the person that I was attracted to.

The topic of homosexuality is not an "issue" to deal with. These are friends, neighbors, and family members with feelings and longings, just like the rest of us. Like me, you may not understand what it's like to be gay, but we can all understand what it means to be attracted to someone. It is a feeling—right or wrong—that comes naturally to us. I was naturally attracted to women, while Michael was naturally attracted to men. It does not mean that these relationships are okay or somehow righteous in God's eyes, but the fact of the matter remains that these were true and genuine feelings.

Our conversation continued, and I began to tell Michael, "Now that I know this about you, it is my responsibility to protect . . ." Michael's fear immediately caused him to stop listening to what I was saying. All that he heard in his mind was, "Now that I know this about you it's my responsibility to protect the church and our children from people like you, you're going to have to step down from ministry or you're going to have to leave the church." But that's not what I said. What I said was, "Michael, now that I know this about you, it is my responsibility to protect you from anyone who would try to hurt you or ostracize you ever again. Jesus loves you, has forgiven you, accepted you, and so you should be at his church. I pray that you can find forgiveness in your heart to forgive those who have hurt you." Michael would go on to say that it was this moment God restored his faith in Jesus and his church.

Jesus Goes to the Hurting and the Marginalized

Homosexuality, same-sex attraction, is a hot topic in our culture right now. As a pastor and student of our culture, I feel an obligation to think clearly and act both truthfully and graciously on this subject. Did I handle this situation correctly? How would Jesus address Michael? Would Jesus condone Michael choosing to live a gay life? Would Jesus condemn Michael? To help us better answer these questions, let's examine who Jesus ministered to and how he goes to the hurting and the marginalized.

The Social Outcast

At the beginning of Jesus's public ministry (after his baptism, temptation, and sermon on the mount), Matthew 8 tells us Jesus went to three marginalized communities. Jesus went first to the leper, then to the centurion guard, and then to Peter's mom—a woman. *"When he came down from the mountain, great crowds followed him. And behold, a leper came to him and knelt before him, saying, "Lord, if you will, you can make me clean"* (Matt. 8:1–2).

Leprosy was a skin disease that caused awful physical afflictions. Leprosy was not only a terrible disease, but it was also defiling; anyone who had it was considered ceremonially unclean and cut off from any religious or social services in the community. Those with leprosy were ostracized and not allowed to live in towns or villages. Not only were they required to keep their distance from people, if they happened to approach anyone, they were required to call out *"Unclean"* (Lev. 13:45).

But the leprous man from the Matthew 8 account had faith to approach Jesus. And Jesus stretched out his hand, touched him, and healed him. Imagine being this man. Ostracized from his community and ordered never to be touched again. As an act of grace, Jesus touched him. He didn't have to touch him to heal him. Jesus could have simply spoken the healing words, but Jesus wants us to see the grace-filled compassion implied when he stretches out his hand and touches this man who has been declared unclean and cast out of the community.

We can learn a lot about Jesus from this encounter. Jesus delights in giving grace to everyone who comes to him. The story of the leprous man is a picture of the gospel. In the Bible, leprosy is always used to describe the terrible and defiling stain and effects of sin that are upon every human. It is our sin that has made us all outsiders. By touching the leper, Jesus demonstrated that he is the one who touches us; he is willing to take our sins upon himself, and he is the one who will become unclean so that we may be healed. Interestingly enough, after Jesus healed this man, he instructed him to go back to the temple to show himself to the priests and offer the gift that Moses commanded. Basically, what Jesus was doing there was inviting him back into fellowship. The one who was ostracized is now clean and welcomed back into the temple.

The Oppressor

"When he had entered Capernaum, a centurion came forward to him, appealing to him, 'Lord, my servant is lying paralyzed at home, suffering terribly'" (Matt. 8:5–6). Jesus heals the leper, who is the ultimate outsider, and now he is approached by a different kind of outsider—a gentile Roman centurion soldier. According to Jewish thinking, this centurion was the wrong race, and he wore the wrong uniform. Here again is a very unusual encounter with Jesus. Roman centurions were loyal to Caesar alone

and known for oppressing the Jewish people, so it is a surprise that he addresses Jesus as Lord, not once but twice in the text. This points to the man's conversion. Only believers call Jesus Lord. For this man to call Jesus Lord is to give up his loyalty to Caesar, and this would've been treason punishable by at the very least, a good beating and imprisonment or at the very worst, death. What stands out as even more unusual is the appeal on behalf of his paralyzed servant who was a slave in his home. This is an unusual request because slaves in the Greco-Roman age were treated with the same regard as animals. If a slave was sick, then the slave owner would kill him and move on. This appeal proved that the centurion was much like Jesus, a loving and compassionate man who wanted the best for his servants. Jesus marveled at this man's faith and responded by saying, *"I will come and heal him"* (Matt. 8:7). Here, Jesus is breaking down cultural barriers by agreeing to go to this Gentile's house. According to Jewish leaders, it was forbidden to enter into a Gentile's house — much like the days of segregation in our own country. There was a time when blacks and whites did not eat in the same places or drink from the same fountains. The same was true between the Jews and the Gentiles. A Jewish person would not dare to be seen in a Gentile's home. Jesus is willing to cross over that line when he says, *"I will come and heal him."*

The Oppressed

"And when Jesus entered Peter's house, he saw his mother-in-law lying sick with a fever. He touched her hand, and the fever left her, and she rose and began to serve him" (Matt. 8:15).

Here, we have another unusual encounter. Jesus heals another religious outcast. First, the leper, then the Gentile Roman soldier's servant, and now a woman. Jesus crosses the barriers of society, race, and now gender. Women in Israel were considered second-class citizens because they were born female. One of the 18 prayers recited by the religious Israelite men each day was a prayer of thanks to God for not being born a woman. Considering that Matthew is writing to a Jewish audience, you can see he wanted to get across very clearly that Jesus came not only for the Jews, but that the Kingdom of Heaven is open to all who believe — the Jew, the outcast, the gentile, the slave, and the oppressed. Jesus heals this woman, and her response was gratitude and worship shown through service. This is the proper response to such a gift. Salvation is for all who call Jesus Lord, and they are to get up to serve him.

The Good News for Outcasts

Now consider who the outcasts are in our culture. Have we created physical, cultural, and sexual barriers in our lives that would keep people from meeting Jesus and feeling welcome in the family of God? Matthew 8 gives us a good argument that Jesus was for the oppressed and marginalized. Jesus loved the outcast and ate with sinners. Jesus was a friend to sinners, and sinners were drawn to Jesus because he was a source of love, grace, mercy, and compassion. By no means did Jesus condone any sinful lifestyle, but at the same time he did not condemn people for their sin either. Here's the good news and the reason why that is true. Jesus's mission was to die and be condemned in our place for all of our sins. In John's Gospel, Jesus tells us in his own words:

> For God so loved the world, that he gave his only Son, that whoever believes in him should not perish but have eternal life. For God did not send his Son into the world to condemn the world, but in order that the world might be saved through him. Whoever believes in him is not condemned, but whoever does not believe is condemned already, because he has not believed in the name of the only Son of God.
>
> John 3:16–18

Sinners and outcasts were drawn to Jesus because he loved them. If there are any people or groups today who have experienced being "outcasts," it is those in the LGBTQ community. In our own context and time, we can confidently say that Jesus would befriend those in this community too, and they would want to spend time with Jesus. Although Jesus associated mostly with the marginalized, the religious leaders of the day did not like this. Unfortunately, this sounds a lot like the Christian church today.

In Luke's Gospel, the Pharisees and scribes (read: pastors and religious scholars) in Jesus's day grumbled that sinners were coming to Jesus. In Luke 15:2, the Pharisees and scribes were criticizing Jesus saying, *"This man receives sinners and eats with them."* To "receive" people in the biblical sense was to welcome them as friends, to accept and associate with them. In Jesus's time, one of the most tangible ways to establish this kind of friendship was to share a meal with people.

To invite a man to a meal was an offer of peace, trust, brotherhood, and forgiveness; in short, sharing a table meant sharing life. Jesus shared his life and was known to hang out with people who lived overtly sinful lifestyles. The best possible news that anyone can hear is that Jesus was a friend to sinners, and that gives us true hope.

Restoring Dignity Value and Worth

This criticism inspired Jesus to tell a series of parables. He talks about three lost things: a lost sheep, a lost coin, and a lost son. There is rich meaning to these parables, which isn't the focus of this chapter. But the end point of the parables is that there is joy over the lost being found. The Pharisees grumbled that this religious teacher, Jesus, was filled with joy to be surrounded by broken people who were lost and found. The Pharisees didn't count sinners as worthy. They thought Jesus's sinner friends needed to look more holy to be counted worthy among the religious community. Imagine the message that sends to someone like my friend Michael who struggles and has felt ostracized in the past. But Jesus welcomes Michael and bestows dignity, value, and worth on him. Every human being, regardless of their particular sin struggle, is made in the image and likeness of God.

The parable of the lost coin teaches us many things, which we won't go into here, but if it teaches us anything, it teaches us how precious we are to God. Jesus says, *"what woman, having ten silver coins, if she loses one coin, does not light a lamp and sweep the house and seek diligently until she finds it? And when she has found it, she calls together*

her friends and neighbors, saying, 'Rejoice with me, for I have found the coin that I had lost'" (Luke 15:8–9).

First, the relationship between the woman and her coin was that of ownership. Even when it was lost, the coin still belonged to her. In the same way, even if we have fallen away or never acknowledged God at all, we all still belong to him by virtue of the fact that God made us. Ironically, in Luke 15, Jesus never makes a distinction between the religious leaders and sinners. He calls them all his sheep. Everyone, no matter our sexual preference, belongs to God and when we finally come to him in repentance, through faith in Jesus Christ, God is getting back what was his all along.

Secondly, the value that this woman placed on her lost coin shows the great value that God places on each and every one of us. As anyone who knows anything about coin collecting can tell you, it's not so much the material of the coin that makes it valuable, but the image that is stamped on it. Take for instance the 1836 U.S. Gobrecht Liberty Seated Silver Dollar. The coin weighs .7734 troy ounce. The last time I looked at the market, silver was valued at $17.34 an ounce. But this coin is valued at more than $110,000. You see, what is significant is not the amount of silver but the image stamped on the coin. If nothing was stamped on that coin, it would be worth about $13, according to a ballpark value of silver at the time of this writing. What makes this coin valuable is the image that is stamped on it. Likewise, we are made in the image and likeness of our King Jesus. Everyone has been stamped with his likeness. We bear a royal image on us, and this gives us tremendous value.

We were made precious when God fashioned us into his image, and this gave us dignity, worth, and value that surpassed all other creatures regardless of our sinful choices. If you struggle with same-sex attraction or you know someone who does, God loves you and has not discarded you. You are precious to him, and he is seeking you.

Stones or Grace?

Like Michael's experience, the message that outcast and marginalized people often hear from the church is that they aren't valued. That they are not welcome because of their sin. But again, what we see in the Gospels over and over is that Jesus welcomes sinners and extends grace to the hurting and the outcast. The woman caught in adultery in John 8 is a prime example.

> *but Jesus went to the Mount of Olives. Early in the morning he came again to the temple. All the people came to him, and he sat down and taught them. The scribes and the Pharisees brought a woman who had been caught in adultery, and placing her in the midst they said to him, "Teacher, this woman has been caught in the act of adultery. Now in the Law Moses commanded us to stone such women. So what do you say?" This they said to test him, that they might have some charge to bring against him. Jesus bent down and wrote with his finger on the ground. And as they continued to ask him, he stood up and said to them, "Let him who is without sin among you be the first to throw a stone at her." And once more he bent down*

and wrote on the ground. But when they heard it, they went away one by one, beginning with the older ones, and Jesus was left alone with the woman standing before him. Jesus stood up and said to her, "Woman, where are they? Has no one condemned you?" She said, "No one, Lord." And Jesus said, "Neither do I condemn you; go, and from now on sin no more."

John 8:1–11

Leveling the Playing Field

The Apostle Paul rebuked the church for judging outsiders. He said, *"For what have I to do with judging outsiders? Is it not those inside the church whom you are to judge?"* (1 Cor. 5:12). Maybe you don't struggle with same-sex attraction, but you do struggle with something—something that's more "acceptable" to the culture. The church has been guilty of using particular issues that we struggle with as Christians—things such as homosexuality—as a platform to make us look better than others. But as soon as we talk about lust, adultery, pornography, gossip, slander, drunkenness, and gluttony, then all of a sudden we want God's grace and forgiveness. Jesus said, that he who is without sin should cast the first stone (John 8:7). We don't know what Jesus was writing in the sand from the above referenced passage, but it compelled the angry mob to drop their stones and walk away. Your sin is just as condemnable as someone who has gay sex. Once we understand how we are more like the Michaels of the world and that we all are desperately in need of God's grace, we will drop our stones and give grace to

77

others. I pray that God will give his people humility and compassion for those who struggle differently than most.

The Good News Is That Jesus Receives Sinners Like You and Me

Church people can be much like the Pharisees. We often see the church as a country club for religious folks rather than a hospital for the sick. The only difference between self-righteous religious know-it-alls and sinners is that sinners know they are lost, and they're able to experience the joy in being found.

When we come to Jesus, no matter our sin, no matter what makes us feel like an outcast, he will take us to himself. This makes what the Pharisees and scribes claimed about Jesus to be one of the most amazing truths in Scripture: *"This man receives sinners and eats with them"* (Luke 15:2). Thank you, Jesus! This means there is an offer of peace, trust, brotherhood, and forgiveness, and that is good news! The Pharisees did not say what they said with joyful praise, however. Instead, it was a criticism. Rather than making their remark with admiration, they made it with condemnation. The Pharisees were shocked to see Jesus hanging out with sinners. As far as they were concerned, the fact that Jesus spent time with outcasts could only mean that Jesus wasn't taking sin seriously enough, or that he was too soft on the sinners. But the very thing they criticize Jesus for was the thing Jesus came to do. He had come to make sinners holy before God. He did not come to condemn sinners; he came to save them. In Jesus's culture—and in ours—having a relationship meant sharing a meal and listening to others, not condemning them.[1]

Now ask yourself this question: Are those who feel outcast and demonized by the Christian community drawn to you because you are like Jesus who was loving, kind, compassionate, graceful, and merciful? Or are you more like the Pharisees and scribes who are only found grumbling? If Jesus were here today, I wonder if maybe the LGBTQ community would also be among the groups of people who want to be near Jesus?

But What about the "Issue" of Homosexuality?

Some readers may object that I haven't addressed this issue adequately. As I said at the beginning of this chapter, it's important to think clearly and act lovingly. I believe that Jesus is Lord over everything, including our sexuality and our relationships. I am not ashamed to admit that I hold to traditional views of sex and marriage—one man and one woman in the confines of a marriage, and any sex outside of God's intended design is a sin. For such sin, Christ has died. The Gospel is good news to the sexual sinner and has the power to transform and save. But again, let's level the playing field; if any sex out of the confines of marriage is a sin, then is there anyone not guilty of this? Just because you may not understand what it's like to be gay and struggle with same-sex attraction, that doesn't mean you need less grace. I also hold firm to the call in 1 Peter which says, *"As obedient children, do not be conformed to the passions of your former ignorance, but as he who called you is holy, you also be holy in all your conduct, since it is written, 'You shall be holy, for I am holy'"* (1 Pet. 1:14–16).

There is grace for all sinners, and we all come equally in need of God's grace. The call from Peter is to live a transformed life in Christ. God's grace that saves us also gives us the power to live holy, transformed, redeemed, joy-filled lives. I asked Michael how the church can love and serve people in the gay community? He said, "By treating them with love and respect, like you would anyone else. Just like Jesus would. Be like Christ. He was a source of love, grace, forgiveness, and compassion. Share the good news about Jesus with them—no matter what their sexual preference is, and trust in the Lord for their salvation, their healing, and their flourishing. Treat them just like you would anyone else."

I will close with a quote from Dr. Preston Sprinkle who said, "We can be right on biblical issues and wrong on love but if we are wrong on love we are wrong altogether."[2]

6

WHY ON EARTH AM I HERE? DOES GOD HAVE A PLAN FOR MY LIFE?

"Thus says the LORD of hosts, the God of Israel, to all the exiles whom I have sent into exile from Jerusalem to Babylon: Build houses and live in them; plant gardens and eat their produce. Take wives and have sons and daughters; take wives for your sons, and give your daughters in marriage, that they may bear sons and daughters; multiply there, and do not decrease. But seek the welfare of the city where I have sent you into exile, and pray to the LORD on its behalf, for in its welfare you will find your welfare. For thus says the LORD of hosts, the God of Israel: Do not let your prophets and your diviners who are among you deceive you, and do not listen to the dreams that they dream, for it is a lie that they are

prophesying to you in my name; I did not send them, declares the LORD. "For thus says the LORD: When seventy years are completed for Babylon, I will visit you, and I will fulfill to you my promise and bring you back to this place. For I know the plans I have for you, declares the LORD, plans for welfare and not for evil, to give you a future and a hope. Then you will call upon me and come and pray to me, and I will hear you. You will seek me and find me, when you seek me with all your heart. I will be found by you, declares the LORD, and I will restore your fortunes and gather you from all the nations and all the places where I have driven you, declares the LORD, and I will bring you back to the place from which I sent you into exile."

Jer. 29:4–14

My wife has worked in the construction field for over 20 years, and every building project begins with an architect who first determines the purpose of the building and how it will be used. This is very important information to know before you draw up the plans to build a building. The general contractor Sheila worked for specialized in building fire stations, which need to be laid out very specifically for safety and efficiency. My son, Daniel, works at a fire station in Rialto, California, and when they get a call, it's almost always an emergency. The layout of their station needs to have a particular flow for fast foot traffic. Also, fire engines with water hoses are parked, and that means drain placement has to be strategic because water drips on the floor. If you don't have drains, the water pools and creates hazards. Likewise, before God created us, he had a specific plan and purpose for our lives. We are created to love and serve God and our neighbors. Knowing this helps us get a picture in our minds to help us answer the questions, "Why on earth am I here, and does God have a plan for my life?"

When God created humans, he declared our purpose from the beginning. We were created to enjoy fellowship with him, to have loving and fruitful relationships with others, and to work and be productive. Mankind was created to multiply and fill the earth with more worshipers of God. This was God's original intent for humanity, and this is what it means to bring glory to God.

But with man's fall into sin (Gen. 3), fellowship with God was broken. Our sin put every relationship to the test because of selfishness and pride. After the fall, work was no longer a joy. Instead, work became hard, stressful, frustrating, and tiresome. Instead of filling the earth with joyful worshippers of God who love and serve their neighbors, we fill the earth with selfish sinners. But there is still hope for us.

We can get back to a place where our lives can bring glory to God. It first begins with being restored to a relationship with our creator, through faith in our Lord and Savior Jesus Christ. Then, our truest sense of meaning and purpose in life will be rediscovered.

In my study of the Scriptures, I found five reasons why we were put on this earth, and I'll use them as an outline for this chapter: (1) we are here to be loved by

God and to love God; (2) we are here to belong to the family of God; (3) we are here to become more like Christ; (4) we are here to work and serve the church; and (5) we are here to carry out a mission for God.

We Are Here to be Loved By God and to Love God

For while we were still weak, at the right time Christ died for the ungodly. For one will scarcely die for a righteous person — though perhaps for a good person one would dare even to die — but God shows his love for us in that while we were still sinners, Christ died for us. Since, therefore, we have now been justified by his blood, much more shall we be saved by him from the wrath of God. For if while we were enemies we were reconciled to God by the death of his Son, much more, now that we are reconciled, shall we be saved by his life. More than that, we also rejoice in God through our Lord Jesus Christ, through whom we have now received reconciliation.

Rom. 5:6–11

According to these verses, God took into account everything there was to know about you, and he still decided to lay his life down for you. Because of the finished work on the cross, nothing will separate you ever again from the love of God. How liberating is that for you? If there's one thing I hope you take away from reading this chapter, it's this: your sin will never take you farther than the grace of God is willing to go. God loves you with an unconditional love. The cross of Christ removes the penalty, the guilt, and the shame caused by sin. When you put your faith securely in Jesus Christ as

Lord and Savior, he removes every barrier between you and your relationship with God. Jesus provided the way to be restored to God so we can have a loving relationship with him.

Early in my walk with Christ, truths like these were hard for me to accept. You wouldn't know it today, but I was bad news in the '90s. The '90s were not only about me abusing drugs, but also about all kinds of bad, and dare I say, evil choices. You didn't have to convince me I was a sinner who deserved the wrath of God. I knew all too well the things I had done and the choices I had made. Not only was I guilty, but I was also ashamed of the things I had done. After all I had done and continued to do, it was hard for me to grasp how God could love a person like me. As I continued to read God's life-giving Word, God began to open my eyes to the gospel—the good news that Jesus took my guilt upon himself and bore my shame on the cross. When Jesus was publicly humiliated, he was beaten, stripped naked, and shamed. This is the most humiliating thing a human being could experience, and I began to see that Jesus was humiliated and shamed in my place. These truths began to open my eyes to the depth of God's love for me. Not only did Jesus take my guilt upon himself and pay the penalty for my sin, he has also set me free from ever feeling ashamed. Jesus has come to forgive sinners and cleanse them of all unrighteousness. In light of this good news, the Apostle Paul said:

What then shall we say to these things? If God is for us, who can be against us? He who did not spare his own Son but gave him up for us all, how will he not also with him graciously give us all things? Who shall bring any charge against God's elect? It is God who justifies. Who is to condemn? Christ Jesus is the one who died—more than that, who was raised—who is at the right hand of God, who indeed is interceding for us. Who shall separate us from the love of Christ? Shall tribulation, or distress, or persecution, or famine, or nakedness, or danger, or sword? As it is written, "For your sake we are being killed all the day long; we are regarded as sheep to be slaughtered." No, in all these things we are more than conquerors through him who loved us. For I am sure that neither death nor life, nor angels nor rulers, nor things present nor things to come, nor powers, nor height nor depth, nor anything else in all creation, will be able to separate us from the love of God in Christ Jesus our Lord.

Rom. 8:31–39

You see, because of Christ, our sin no longer separates us from the love of God. As Jesus said in John 15:9, *"As the Father has loved me, so have I loved you. Abide in my love."* When Jesus calls us to abide in his love, he is calling us to rest deeply in the fact that we are loved unconditionally. So what does it mean to "abide?" I love to cook, and there is nothing better than a good marinade. When you marinate a piece of meat, you start by completely submerging it into your favorite sauce; then, over time the flavor penetrates the entire piece of meat. This is what it means to "abide." Jesus wants us to abide in his love— not moving too quickly from this truth, just abiding, taking our time to let his love for us penetrate every aspect of our being.

These truths are for all who place their faith in Jesus Christ. This is the love that Jesus wants us to abide in. Not only are we forgiven, loved, and reconciled to God, but we are also reconciled to God's family—the church.

We Are Here to Belong to the Family of God

All of us are looking for a place to belong, a place where we can feel love and acceptance. We have this desire because God created us with a longing in our souls to belong in community with one another. He gave us this longing because God's purpose in creating us was for us to become members of his eternal family. As we read in Ephesians:

> *Blessed be the God and Father of our Lord Jesus Christ, who has blessed us in Christ with every Spiritual blessing in the heavenly places, even as he chose us in him before the foundation of the world, that we should be holy and blameless before him. In love he predestined us for adoption as sons through Jesus Christ, according to the purpose of his will.*
>
> Eph. 1:3–5

In 1997, my addiction and the community I was hanging out in landed me in a jail cell. This put me into another community called the "first offenders tank." This was not the kind of community I had in mind. It was like a locker room full of 40 or 50 men in a small space. I had no patience with those men and no desire to be there. I remember asking one of the old-timers,

"How do you get out of here?" He said, "There's two ways. You get released, or you get in a fight and get sent to the 'hole.'" He was right. As fate would have it, my stupidity landed me in the hole. The guards came in, arrested me, and placed me in a single-man cell where I was segregated for 23 hours a day. There I was, stripped from all community. The locker-room feel of the first offenders tank was unmanageable, but this was even worse.

While I was in confinement, I came to my senses and said to myself, "I'm done." Sheila was there to pick me up when I was released from jail in March 1998. My life of drugs and crime was over. We separated ourselves from that community and started a family together. In 2002, Sheila and I placed our faith in Jesus and became part of God's family—his church.

God created us to live in his community—the church. In Genesis 2, God said it is not good that man should be alone. Sadly, people both inside and outside the church are lonely. We need relationships because God has designed us to live together. Colossians tells us,

Put on then, as God's chosen ones, holy and beloved, compassionate hearts, kindness, humility, meekness, and patience, bearing with one another and, if one has a complaint against another, forgiving each other; as the Lord has forgiven you, so you also must forgive.

Col. 3:12–14

In my life, God used severe circumstances to send me into a community that I shouldn't be part of. Through that process, he brought me into his community. Ultimately, it's God's will and purpose for us to become members of his eternal family. Not only are we restored to God through faith in Christ, but we are also restored to one another. The life of a follower of Christ is so much more than just believing; it is also about belonging. So we are here to love God and belong to the family of God.

We Are Here to Become More Like Christ

Our third purpose in this life is to become more like Christ. But we often set our bars a little low, don't we? As a newer Christian, I got involved with a motorcycle ministry. There were many good people in that community, but it had a bit of a "Christianity-lite" kind of feel to it. I remember calling my dad and telling him all about this great ministry and community. I told him I was headed for leadership, and he said, "Well, that's good, Mike. But it's really easy to feel good about yourself when you're hanging around a bunch of dummies." My dad's point wasn't to put down the good people I was in community with. The takeaway truth of what he said was that whoever you are, all Christians are to set their focus on Jesus. Of course, we need others to see Jesus clearly and model his godly character, but we set our sights on him, not on the low bar of how we're going to fit into a given community.

God has saved us for the purpose of transforming us into the likeness of his son, Jesus. Romans says it like this, *"Do not be conformed to this world, but be transformed by the renewal of your mind, that by testing you may discern what is the will of God, what is good and acceptable and perfect"* (Rom. 12:2). The reason we are called to transformation is in order to love and serve others like Christ has served us.

But some of us may be asking ourselves, how do we renew our minds in the first place? We do this by teaching one another through intentional discipleship relationships. In Proverbs, it says that iron sharpens iron, and one man sharpens another (Prov. 27:17). In the Great Commission (Matt. 28:18–20), Jesus calls us to make disciples by teaching others everything he commanded. In his own life, Jesus himself modeled for us how to love, serve, and care for one another. He shows us how to face loneliness, temptation, criticism, suffering, and so much more. The Apostle Paul picked up on this discipleship idea when he instructed Timothy: *"You then, my child, be strengthened by the grace that is in Christ Jesus, and what you have heard from me in the presence of many witnesses entrust to faithful men who will be able to teach others also"* (2 Tim. 2:1–2).

When I came to Encounter Church, there was an underlying fear that I was going to drive out the older, more mature believers. But the truth is, the older believers had attracted me to this church. We have church members who have been married for 50 years. These are the kind of people I want discipling me. We need God's people in our lives to learn what it means to walk in faith with Jesus in the context of a loving marriage. God has blessed our churches with faithful men and women who are more than willing to disciple one another. Connect and spend time with another believer, and get discipled so you can grow to be more like Christ.

We Are to Work and Serve the Church

God created each of us to work and serve one another. *"For we are his workmanship, created in Christ Jesus for good works, which God prepared beforehand, that we should walk in them"* (Eph. 2:10). Each of us is created and saved for the good works for which God has uniquely gifted us. My friend Dave Kraft once told me something very true: as a leader, I should work in my giftedness and staff in my weaknesses. This was simple but profound advice. It's best for me to spend my energy doing the things I'm gifted in, and enlist the help of others where I am weak so they can be used by God, too. We are not created to operate in this life alone, but I believe together with God's help, we can do everything he is calling us to do.

There are many examples of how the church comes together as the body of Christ, and often it's not in our competencies and strengths, but in our weakness. A dear friend of ours suffers from debilitating chronic pain. One day she said, "I know I'm part of the body of Christ, but I kind of feel like the appendix." It was as if she was saying she felt useless because she is in bed so much. But let me tell you, she is a prayer warrior and one of the most encouraging people I've ever known. She understands her own need for God because of her troubles, and she spends many, many hours in prayer. She also knows—even when others don't—that we all need prayer all the time! I do pray to God that she gets healed, but she is a vital part of the body of Christ even in her debilitated condition. The devil can come in and say we're insignificant. That's a lie from the pit of hell.

Don't believe it. You are significant, and there is no one in the body of Christ who is not an essential part of the body of Christ.

We Are Here to Be on Mission for God

In a recent preaching series at our church, we challenged our congregation toward evangelism. We began our campaign by asking the question, "Who's in your circle?" We are calling our congregation to consider the people that God has placed in their circle of influence. This could be family, friends, workmates, teammates, classmates, and the like. The call is to identify them by writing their names down on a bookmark that we provided. The next step is to pray for these people daily, asking God to draw them to himself, and cause them to sense their need for Jesus. The final step is toward Christlikeness. The call is for the church to love, serve, and sacrifice for the people in our circles unconditionally. This is what we believe Christ has done for us. We believe, in faith, that God will draw these people to himself and that he will convict them of their sin and their need for a Savior. And when they see Jesus for the first time, they will recognize him immediately because they first saw him in us.

There is nothing more rewarding and fulfilling than to be used by God to see people come to faith in Jesus Christ. Just as God sent Jesus into the world to save us, Jesus sends us into the world to live as he lived, to love as he loved, and to bring more people into the family of God. We are here not only to serve our fellow believers, but we are also called to be on a mission for the sake of those who don't yet believe in Jesus. Luke's Gospel tells us that Jesus, *"came to seek and to save the lost"* (Luke 19:10). Speaking to the Father in heaven, Jesus prayed, *"As you sent me into the world, so I have sent them into the world"* (John 17:18).

This "them" that Jesus is speaking of is us! Jesus is sending us into the world to share the gospel. There can be a lot of fear attached to being on a mission for Jesus. Why is that? For one, we fear rejection. The truth is that most people would come to church if they were simply invited. I believe that people are far more receptive to hearing the gospel from a friend than a stranger.

But some of us may fear the feeling of coming across like a salesperson. God is not asking you to sell anything. The Holy Spirit is the one who convicts a sinner of the need for a Savior, and it is the Holy Spirit who applies the work of Jesus in that person's life. We are simply called to love our neighbor like Christ and share the good news about Jesus.

Some of us may also fear looking foolish because our lives are not all put together. What's true of us all, though, is that everybody is in-process. No one in the church is perfect. Think about it this way: You're not witnessing about you; you're witnessing to the goodness of Jesus, and how he has come to save broken and weak people like yourself. God refused to remove Paul's weakness in an effort to keep him humble. And this is what the Lord declared to Paul:

My grace is sufficient for you, for my power is made perfect in weakness. Therefore I will boast all the more gladly of my weaknesses, so that the power of

93

Christ may rest upon me. For the sake of Christ, then, I am content with weaknesses, insults, hardships, persecutions, and calamities. For when I am weak, then I am strong.

2 Cor. 12:9–10

Another fear some of us have in common is that sometimes we don't know how to share the gospel. But one of the best things we can do is live our lives in such a way that they testify to our love for Jesus and that everything the Bible says about Jesus is true. I do believe we should live righteously, but in reality our sin and imperfections are often opportunities to boast more about Jesus's grace. In his book *Friend of Sinners*, Harvey Turner writes:

Daily we need to evangelize ourselves. Our righteousness is in Jesus! He lived for us. He obeyed the commands of God perfectly on our behalf. He died in our place for sins. He rose that we might be new and receive the Holy Spirit! Our past, present, and future failures or success no longer define us. Jesus's past, present, and future defines our reality and gives us our identity. Jesus one day will heal this broken world and all that makes us weep. We are now a citizen of his kingdom! It is finished! Jesus has done all that you will ever need! God accepts you! God likes you! God loves you! You're now adopted into his family!" Preach the gospel to yourself in joy, pain, and despair. Preach the gospel to yourself even when you sin, when you feel shame, guilt, and doubt, when you succeed, and when you fail. Let the gospel be the home where you live.[1]

Conclusion

When we consider the question of why we exist, there are thousands of competing voices. Our culture tells us we need to be significant, so we can somehow make a mark on the world. The actor Jim Carrey once said, "I wish everyone could experience being rich and famous so they could better understand that's not the path to a better life."[2] Instead, what we see from the example of Jesus is how he loves God and loves others. Jesus lays down his life for the sake of others, and that's what we're called to as well.

When we consistently fill our hearts and minds with the good news of Jesus, that love will naturally overflow into the lives of the people that God has placed in our circles of influence. We are here to love God; to be committed to love, care for, and serve one another in community; to disciple one another to become more like Jesus; and to be on a mission together so more people can come to know, love, follow, and serve Jesus Christ. The gospel of Jesus is the only gift you can give someone that will last for an eternity. It is certainly the most loving gift a person will ever receive. And to pass on that gift to others seems to me to be the most profoundly meaningful thing we could ever exist for.

7

WHY ARE THERE SO MANY RELIGIONS?

For the wrath of God is revealed from heaven against all ungodliness and unrighteousness of men, who by their unrighteousness suppress the truth. For what can be known about God is plain to them, because God has shown it to them. For his invisible attributes, namely, his eternal power and divine nature, have been clearly perceived, ever since the creation of the world, in the things that have been made. So they are without excuse. For although they knew God, they did not honor him as God or give thanks to him, but they became futile in their thinking, and their foolish hearts were darkened. Claiming to be wise, they became fools, and exchanged the glory of the immortal God for images resembling mortal man and birds and animals and creeping things. Therefore God gave them up in the lusts of their hearts to impurity,

*to the dishonoring of their bodies among themselves,
because they exchanged the truth about God for a lie
and worshiped and served the creature rather than
the Creator, who is blessed forever! Amen.*

Rom. 1:18–25

Seeking Truth and Understanding

At the age of nine, Brent's parents decided it was important, for their relationship and family, to travel. They moved to eastern Australia. For Brent, this was the beginning of a lifelong journey. Brent attended an all-boys Catholic school where it was difficult for him to fit in. The lesson was, learn to adapt. After a few years in Australia, his parents decided to venture on to Southeast Asia, living in Singapore and then Jakarta, Indonesia. From that point, they decided for health reasons and Brent's education to move back to a Western society. They moved to Switzerland and then to Germany for a year, all of this by the time Brent turned 15. Needless to say, Brent had been immersed in many cultures and lifestyles at an early age.

In the summer of 2017, Sheila and I attended the memorial service for George Bethell, the father of our dear friends Ryan and Tricia Bethell. It was there that I met George's nephew, Brent. Brent is now a 55-year-old cattle rancher in Eustace, Texas. This caught me completely by surprise because Brent is not your stereotypical cowboy. If I were to guess, I would have easily said he was from Orange County, California. No cowboy hat or chewing tobacco here. I would soon find out that Brent was originally from Northern California.

We introduced ourselves, and Brent asked me what I do for a living and, when I told him I was a pastor, my guess is that he was equally surprised by the way I looked. (Not your typical pastor.)

As the conversation went on, Brent shared with me that he is a "seeker of truth and understanding." And at the age of 17, he decided to go his own way. Brent said, "I was attracted and intrigued by business and money." He reasoned that people with money and success had freedom and privilege. So he worked hard as an entrepreneur finding his way in business. Brent was successful in business and relationships for many years until everything literally came crumbling down in the 1989 earthquakes in Northern California. This caused major damage to his business and residence. He was also going through some relationship downturns at the time. It was a perfect storm. Brent began to question his life and purpose. He sensed an emptiness inside. So he liquidated his assets and set out on a journey to seek what this life was all about. He visited many of the places where he had traveled with his parents as a youngster. Reconnecting with his past friendships was of particular interest to him. He wanted to see what those connections were about. He also spent time in India hoping to better understand his spiritual side, which continued to tug at him.

In his quest for truth and understanding, Brent wanted answers to questions such as these: What does it mean to be fulfilled? What are people searching for? What am I searching for? What do I really want for myself? What causes me to think or feel the way I do? Am I a product of my upbringing and the influences around me, or do

I have free will? I have a need to belong, how does this affect me and influence my decision making? What are other people's needs and how do those needs affect their lives? All of these and many other questions are what made Brent into what he called a watcher, an observer, and a seeker of truth and understanding of himself and others. These questions and more are why so many religions and ideologies exist today.

We All Suppress the Truth

The Bible says all of us want to know the truth about our lives and our purpose, but understanding and accepting that truth is limited because of our fallen nature. This causes us to suppress the truth. Everyone has suppressed the truth—Christians included. When Paul wrote his doctrine in Romans 1, he wasn't just speaking about all the bad people out there. He's talking about the entire human race—every human being. Because of their sin—our sin—we have suppressed the truth about God, and we are guilty of suppressing the truth in the church today.

The church is also without excuse. We have the Scripture, but we replace God with gods of our own liking because it's much easier to deal with a god that we can control and manipulate. I am guilty of this too. My sin and my problems look so much better in my mind than in God's Word. In our self-righteous thinking, we create images of a god in our mind who accepts and loves everyone, because we do not want to carry any blame for our sin.

All religions believe we are to live a certain way. Christians believe that too, but we don't believe we can earn our salvation. Christianity is not about doing the right thing, it's all about having the right relationship. This is so much different from simply trying hard to be good or having to satisfy a false god's demand through religious duties.

Many followers of the world's other religions seek to solve the problem of righteousness and morality by themselves. They believe that they can cooperate with their god(s) to live up to the demands of righteousness. However, Christians believe it is our sin that separates us from God and that the consequence of our sin is death. Because of our sin, we are unable to please God or save ourselves. We also believe God loves us and has decided to send us a Savior. We don't save us. Jesus is the one who saves us.

Jesus is the Son of God who came to earth to take the punishment that we deserved for sin. Jesus died and rose from the dead. If, by faith, you believe in Jesus as your Savior, trusting in his death alone, there is full payment for your sins; you will be forgiven, saved, justified, redeemed, and reconciled to God. It does not matter where you were born, what nationality you are, or by what religion or ideology you characterize yourself. It is in Christ that all people find their true identity and purpose.

Jesus Is the Truth

Our search for truth and understanding does not have to stop. But the who and the where we go to find truth is what is important. Jesus said, *"I am the way, and the truth, and the life"* (John 14:6).

According to Jesus, truth is more than a collection of thoughts and principles; truth is who he is. Scripture tells us, if we have been raised with Christ, we are to seek the things that are above, where Christ is seated at the right hand of God. We are to set our minds on things that are above, not on things that are on earth (Col. 3:1–3).

Contending for the Faith

One of the questions I was asked was, "Why do the three major religions—Christianity, Judaism, and Islam—fight so much?" Regardless of religion or background, we all love our family and friends. Because people of other religions love their family and friends too, they want them to believe in the "truth" as they see it. We Christians believe there is only one way to heaven and it is through Christ Jesus. Because we believe this and because we love people, we contend with people about the truth of this claim. But those who live according to another religion or other ideology have their truth claims too, and that means they will contend for their beliefs because they love their friends and family. People of differing beliefs fight for what they believe is true, just like we Christians fight for the souls of men and women.

Every religion addresses a basic set of questions such as: Where did man come from? Why are we here? Is there life after death? Is there a God? If there is a God, how can I know him? There are many different ways to answer these questions, depending on your ideology or religion. And each ideology produces a set of lenses—a worldview—through which people see the whole world. These worldviews inevitably create competing truth claims, and this can create hostility among people. But in keeping with Paul's argument, we Christians are also guilty of hostility. We too have suppressed the truth. Historically, the Christian Church has led the charge on violence against others. Today, we tend to point our fingers at all the bad guys out there in the world as if we're the "good guys." But Christians have been guilty of shedding much blood in the name of Jesus. Christians need to be reminded of the words of St. Augustine of Hippo who apparently said, "The truth is like a lion. You don't have to defend it. Let it loose and it will defend itself." Christians need to be reminded that divisiveness and violence are never the answer. Rather, it is the preaching and teaching of God's holy Word and unleashing the love and good news of Jesus that establishes the truth in a person's heart.

Christians Are to Be Characterized by Peace

Listen to what Jesus says about peace in John 14:27: *"Peace I leave with you. My peace I give you, not as the world gives you, I give to you. Let not your hearts be troubled. Neither let them be afraid."*

Jesus tells us in John 16:33, *"I have said these things to you, that in me you have peace. In the world you will have tribulation but take heart. I have overcome the world."* In John 20:21, Jesus says to the disciples again, *"Peace be with you. As the Father has sent me, even so I am sending you."* Again, Jesus says, *"Blessed are the peacemakers for they shall be called sons of God"* (Matt. 5:9).

Being Peacemakers

If you are a Christian, I would encourage you to be a peacemaker among the people that God has put in your life. The best way we can help bring peace into others' lives is to introduce them to the Prince of Peace, Jesus Christ. Speaking to the Corinthian church, the Apostle Paul shares that his responsibility is to simply share the good news of Jesus Christ, and the Holy Spirit does all the saving and transforming. He says:

And I, when I came to you, brothers, did not come proclaiming to you the testimony of God with lofty speech or wisdom. For I decided to know nothing among you except Jesus Christ and him crucified. And I was with you in weakness and in fear and much trembling, and my speech and my message were not in plausible words of wisdom, but in demonstration of the Spirit and of power, so that your faith might not rest in the wisdom of men but in the power of God. Yet among the mature we do impart wisdom, although it is not a wisdom of this age or of the rulers of this age, who are doomed to pass away. But we impart a secret and hidden wisdom of God, which God decreed before the ages for our glory. None of the rulers of this age understood this, for if they had, they would not have crucified the Lord of glory. But, as it is written, "What no eye has seen, nor ear heard, nor the heart of man imagined, what God has prepared for those who love him"—these things God has revealed to us through the Spirit. For the Spirit searches everything, even the depths of God. For who knows a person's thoughts except the Spirit of that person, which is in him? So also no one comprehends the thoughts of God except the Spirit of God.

1 Cor. 2:1–11

If you have friends who have different beliefs, trust in the Lord for them. Love, serve, and sacrifice for them unconditionally. Develop some relational equity with them. Relational equity is like financial equity; it gives you leverage to do something significant and, in this case, you get to share the truth about Jesus Christ. There is nothing more significant than that![1] With God's help, we will see many of the people in our circles of influence come to faith in Jesus! Let others know we want to be their friend and get to know them.

Do All Religions Lead to God?

The short answer is, yes, every religion will lead to God. Unfortunately, that is not good news. In Philippians, Paul writes,

God has highly exalted him [Jesus] and bestowed on him the name that is above every name, so that at the name of Jesus every knee should bow, in heaven and on earth and under the earth, and every tongue confess that Jesus Christ is Lord, to the glory of God the Father.

Phil. 2:9–11

According to this scripture, every person who has ever existed, from the beginning of time to the end of time, will bow and confess that Jesus Christ is Lord and that the name of Jesus is above every name. That means his name is above the name of Judaism, Buddhism, Islam, Hinduism, Mormonism, Atheism, Agnosticism, Satanism, and every other "ism." Jesus's name is above every race, every creed, every color, and every tribe. There will be those who place their faith in Jesus and bow to him as Lord and Savior and receive their inheritance and reward in heaven. And tragically, there will be those who will face judgment for not placing their faith in his finished work on the cross. This is why it is so important for Christians to share the truth about Jesus Christ with the people that God has placed in their lives. The good news is God is patient and he is delaying the day of final judgment so more people can come to faith in the one true God.

A Gospel That Flows from Our Lives

As the world grows increasingly diverse, we have a wonderful opportunity to see many come to faith in Jesus. This is a great question to ask because we all have friends in our circle of influence that embrace different religions. The barrier of religion and race is not too big for God to cross. God's desire for Christians is to use us to share the truth about Jesus Christ. Jesus said people will know Christians by our love for one another. The marks of a true Christian are found in Romans 12:

> Let love be genuine. Abhor what is evil; hold fast to what is good. Love one another with brotherly affection. Outdo one another in showing honor. Do not be slothful in zeal, be fervent in Spirit, serve the Lord. Rejoice in hope, be patient in tribulation, be

constant in prayer. Contribute to the needs of the saints and seek to show hospitality. Bless those who persecute you; bless and do not curse them. Rejoice with those who rejoice, weep with those who weep. Live in harmony with one another. Do not be haughty, but associate with the lowly. Never be wise in your own sight. Repay no one evil for evil, but give thought to do what is honor able in the sight of all. If possible, so far as it depends on you, live peaceably with all. Beloved, never avenge yourselves, but leave it to the wrath of God, for it is written, "Vengeance is mine, I will repay, says the Lord." To the contrary, "if your enemy is hungry, feed him; if he is thirsty, give him something to drink; for by so doing you will heap burning coals on his head." Do not be overcome by evil, but overcome evil with good.

Rom. 12:9–21

Historically, this kind of love has not always characterized the Christian Church. But more importantly, we should ask the question, does this characterize me? You don't have to have a degree to love people. Pray and ask God to use you to love the people that he has placed in your life. Love them unconditionally, no strings attached. It's that kind of love that will testify to Jesus's love. Pray for your friends every day, asking God to draw them to himself. Pray that they will sense God's presence in a real way. Pray that God will open their eyes to see their need for him. Pray that God will use you to touch the lives of others no matter their race or religion. By God's amazing grace, I believe we can see every tribe, tongue, and nation confessing faith in Jesus and being baptized into the family of God and filled with the Holy Spirit.

Conclusion

There are so many people like my new friend, Brent, the Texan cattle rancher, who are seekers of truth and understanding. This kind of authenticity is what people need to see in our lives. It makes the gospel believable. If you can live your life with a Romans 12 mindset, it will open the door for people to want to ask about the hope that you have in Jesus. Jesus is not inviting us into another religion; he invites us into a relationship. It is in this relationship that we find forgiveness for sin as well as reconciliation with the one true God and with the family of God. My prayer is that God will give us more opportunities to meet seekers of truth and understanding like my new friend, Brent. Again, truth is more than a collection of thoughts and principles; truth is a person, and his name is Jesus. My prayer for Brent is that the gospel will take root in his heart, so he can rest from his wandering, because he will have found the truth and understanding he is searching for in Jesus.

8

WHY DID GOD FLOOD THE EARTH?

The LORD saw that the wickedness of man was great in the earth, and that every intention of the thoughts of his heart was only evil continually. And the LORD regretted that he had made man on the earth, and it grieved him to his heart. So the LORD said, "I will blot out man whom I have created from the face of the land, man and animals and creeping things and birds of the heavens, for I am sorry that I have made them." But Noah found favor in the eyes of the LORD. These are the generations of Noah. Noah was a righteous man, blameless in his generation. Noah walked with God. And Noah had three sons, Shem, Ham, and Japheth. Now the earth was corrupt in God's sight, and the earth was filled with violence. And God saw the earth, and behold, it was corrupt, for all flesh had corrupted their way on the earth. And God said to Noah, "I have

*determined to make an end of all flesh, for the earth is
filled with violence through them. Behold, I will destroy
them with the earth.*

Gen. 6:5–13

B efore going into full-time ministry, I was a safety
manager for a trucking company owned by
my good friend, Jerry Butcher. Jerry taught me
everything I knew about transportation safety, which is
twofold. First, we had to be compliant with all the federal,
state, and local agencies. Our drivers had to meet all the
standards to qualify to drive a commercial motor vehicle.
Also, our equipment needed to be regularly maintained.
The second and most important factor was the safety of
our drivers. Jerry allowed me to handpick my trainers,
and I had some of the top drivers in the company on my
team. These employees were dedicated to the company.
They understood their responsibilities—which included
operating a vehicle weighing up to 80,000 pounds. After
new hires were brought onto the team, they were assigned
to trainers who ensured they performed their duties
safely and professionally. Once fully trained, drivers were
released to drive independently and trusted to do their
job. But no matter how good our training was, we were
never fully able to prevent incidents from happening.

Everything stopped when a call came in about a
driver who was in a collision or injured while on the
job. My first priority was the driver's safety. Once I was
certain the driver was going to be okay, I would begin an
investigation to determine the cause of the incident. If the
driver was at fault, we would determine the best course of

action. The minimum action was three days off and extra training, and the maximum was immediate termination. It all depended on the severity of the incident. If the mistake was too severe to let that driver continue to drive for the company, I would have to let that person go.

What does all this have to do with the flood in the days of Noah? Let me try to explain. Every time I terminated an employee, it was the right thing to do. Yet I always felt regret and grief when doing it. I felt regret for hiring that person in the first place or regret for not training that driver better. I thought to myself, if I had never hired them or if I had trained them better, these incidents wouldn't have happened. I would also feel grief knowing this particular incident was so bad that the only responsible thing to do was terminate the driver's employment. Even though I felt regret and grief, I knew it was still the right thing to do. It would have been irresponsible for me and the company to allow that person to continue to drive knowing the risk to themselves or others. Maybe you're responsible for things and people in your life, and you've experienced regret and grief, too. Athough these tough decisions aren't on the level of making the decision to judge the world, in a small way, they help us understand the heart of God when trying to answer these questions: Why did God flood the earth? Why did God judge the world so severely? Genesis 6 gives us some reasons.

Why Did God Flood the Earth?

In Genesis, Moses tells us a tragic story of God's regret and grief, and Genesis 6 gives us details about why God sent the flood. God's judgment may seem severe, but consider the following four things. Mankind was wicked, their thoughts were always evil, their intentions were always corrupt, and the earth was filled with violence (Gen. 6:5–12). This description of humanity as corrupt and evil is completely different from the description of humanity given just five chapters earlier in Genesis 1, when all creation was at peace. With that in mind, let's reflect on the goodness and intention for God's creation and what went wrong.

When God completed his creation, he declared it was *"very good"* (Gen. 1:31). The crowning achievement of God's creation was mankind because he created humanity uniquely in his image and likeness. In the Garden of Eden, Adam and Eve were called to be devoted to God and to one another. They were called to work, take care of the earth, be fruitful, and fill the earth with more worshipers of God. The Lord gave Adam and Eve everything they needed to flourish and be successful. In the middle of the garden was the tree of the knowledge of good and evil from which God had forbidden them to eat. Out of love for them, God warned them of the consequence of their disobedience. He said, *"the day that you eat of it you shall surely die"* (Gen. 2:17).

By Genesis 3, both Adam and Eve were deceived. Satan convinced them that they wouldn't die and that they could be just like God, knowing good from evil. The Scripture says,

> *So when the woman saw that the tree was good for food, and that it was a delight to the eyes, and that the tree was to be desired to make one wise, she took of its*

fruit and ate, and she also gave some to her husband who was with her, and he ate.

Gen. 3:6

Immediately, they felt something they'd never felt before—the guilt and shame of sin. Adam and Eve began to feel, see, and experience the things that God had warned them of and protected them from.

Fast forward 10 generations later, in Genesis 6, and what God had originally declared to be good in the garden became so wicked, so evil, so corrupt, so violent that he felt it was necessary to blot out an entire generation from the face of the earth. We're told the Lord regretted that he'd made man and that he was grieved in his heart. But this is not the regret you feel when you realize you have made a mistake.

God sorrowfully regretted that all he had originally intended to be good had been poisoned by sin. His heart broke, and he was sorrowful for the way mankind turned out. What he intended for good was used for the spread of evil. Over 10 generations, their sin led to wickedness, evil, corruption, and violence. God's solution was to cleanse the earth, remove the problem, and start over. It was the most sensible thing to do, and it would have been irresponsible for God to let such wickedness continue. But also consider God's love and intention for mankind.

On a human level, we really don't have a category to fully understand this kind of regret and grief. But we do have real-life scenarios that can help us begin to understand this regret and sorrow. As I said before, as a safety manager of the trucking company, it would be irresponsible for me to put certain people back to work. But let's pretend that I knew of an employee who wanted to harm people on the highway and use our truck as a battering ram. For me to allow that person to continue to drive would be absolutely irresponsible, and I would be the one who needed to be fired. Likewise, God's solution may seem severe, but when we consider the level of wickedness, evil, and corruption that mankind had stooped to, it would have been irresponsible for God not to do something. So God saw fit to cleanse the earth. Maybe instead of purely seeing this as an act of judgment, we could also consider it as an act of God's grace.

God's Grace

What's perhaps more surprising about this tragic story is God's grace. Noah's generation—much like our own—deserved the judgment of God because of their sin and disobedience. But judgment isn't the last word. Weaved into the ugliness of sin and the promise of judgment is the grace and mercy of God. In Genesis 6:8–9, we read: *"But Noah found favor in the eyes of the LORD. These are the generations of Noah. Noah was a righteous man, blameless in his generation. Noah walked with God."*

Notice that verse 8 reads, *"Noah found favor in the eyes of the Lord."* When we read this, we need to understand that Noah was just as guilty as the rest of mankind. When God looked down upon the earth and saw mankind's continual wicked, evil, corrupt, and violent ways, he didn't exclude Noah from that terrible list. You see, Noah was a sinner like everyone else, and he deserved the same judgment that all of the men and women of his generation received. Noah didn't escape God's judgment because of anything he had earned. We often think in terms of "you get what you deserve," and that makes its way into how we think about God too. But that's not how things work with God.

The word *favor* here doesn't mean God met Noah halfway. Favor translated from the Hebrew word *hēn* means "grace." And the definition of "grace" is the unmerited favor and love of God. This is why we can say that when Noah found favor in the eyes of the Lord, we can also say he found the free, unmerited grace and love of God. The only reason Noah was "blameless in his time" was because he found favor and grace with God. God chose to grace Noah with righteousness. This is what left him blameless, not his own goodness. Not only was Noah considered blameless in God's sight, he was also saved from judgment through the building of the ark.

Noah's Rescue and Our Rescue

In Genesis 6:13–22, God gave Noah detailed instructions on how to build the ark. The ark was a tangible gift of God's grace that provided safety for Noah, his family, and all the various animals. When the ark was finished and the animals came to Noah, God closed the door and flooded the earth. As the story goes, after 40 days and 40 nights, the waters subsided to reveal dry land and, by God's grace, Noah and his family were saved (Gen. 7:12–24).

Then Noah built an altar to the LORD and took some of every clean animal and some of every clean bird and offered burnt offerings on the altar. And when the

LORD *smelled the pleasing aroma, the* LORD *said in his heart, "I will never again curse the ground because of man, for the intention of man's heart is evil from his youth. Neither will I ever again strike down every living creature as I have done."*

Gen. 8:20–21

So what does any of this have to do with us, today? Just this: Jesus Christ became our ark. The bad news is that like Noah, mankind is still as sinful as it ever was. Romans 3 tells us, *"None is righteous, no, not one; no one understands; no one seeks for God. All have turned aside; together they have become worthless; no one does good, not even one"* (Rom. 3:10–12). The Apostle Peter also tells us,

But the day of the Lord will come like a thief, and then the heavens will pass away with a roar, and the heavenly bodies will be burned up and dissolved, and the earth and the works that are done on it will be exposed.

2 Pet. 3:10

This means that just as in the days of Noah, God will judge the world again, but this time with fire. But the good news is that just as God did in the days of Noah, he has provided us with a way of escape from this judgment.

The story of Noah points us forward to the cross and the gospel of Jesus Christ. Our rescue is found in the life, death, and resurrection of Jesus Christ. It is through Jesus that we, like Noah, find *"favor in the eyes of the Lord"* (Gen. 6:8), not because of something that we have done to earn it. God gave detailed plans to Noah when building the ark, which became what God used to save Noah and his family. In the same way, God planned out every detail of Jesus's life. God sent Jesus Christ to take our judgment for us, and he died in our place.

In Jesus's time, a religious leader named Nicodemus came to him and asked Jesus what he must do to be saved. Jesus told him he must be born again.

For God did not send his Son into the world to condemn the world, but in order that the world might be saved through him. Whoever believes in him is not condemned, but whoever does not believe is condemned already, because he has not believed in the name of the only Son of God. And this is the judgment: the light has come into the world, and people loved the darkness rather than the light because their works were evil.

John 3:17–19

Likewise, the Apostle Paul shares the good news with us in Romans 10 when he says,

Everyone who believes in him will not be put to shame. For there is no distinction between Jew and Greek; for the same Lord is Lord of all, bestowing his riches on all who call on him. For everyone who calls on the name of the Lord will be saved.

Rom. 10:11–13

In our time and place, our day of judgment draws closer every single day. So, we must take the words of Jesus in the Gospel of Luke seriously:

Just as it was in the days of Noah, so will it be in the days of the Son of Man. They were eating and drinking and marrying and being given in marriage, until the day when Noah entered the ark, and the flood came and destroyed them all. Likewise, just as it was in the days of Lot—they were eating and drinking, buying and selling, planting and building, but on the day when Lot went out from Sodom, fire and sulfur rained from heaven and destroyed them all—so will it be on the day when the Son of Man is revealed. On that day, let the one who is on the housetop, with his goods in the house, not come down to take them away, and likewise let the one who is in the field not turn back. Remember Lot's wife. Whoever seeks to preserve his life will lose it, but whoever loses his life will keep it.

Luke 17:26–33

Conclusion

The Apostle Peter described Noah as a herald of righteousness (2 Peter 2:5). Noah preached to his people, and they had the opportunity to climb aboard the ark and be saved. But the people rejected that opportunity to receive grace and be saved. Instead, they were swallowed up in the waters of God's judgment. You don't have to be like them. God is offering you a way of escape, too. Today, everyone who calls on the name of Jesus can be saved. You can find favor in the eyes of the LORD. Like Noah, you can be made righteous and declared blameless when you place your faith in the life, death, and resurrection of Jesus Christ.

9

IF GOD IS SO POWERFUL, WHY IS THERE SUFFERING?

By Tim Gilman

"Once God has spoken; twice have I heard this: that power belongs to God" (Ps. 62:11).

"Behold, these are but the outskirts of his ways, and how small a whisper do we hear of him! But the thunder of his power who can understand?" (Job 26:14).

"Let the groans of the prisoners come before you; according to your great power, preserve those doomed to die!" (Ps. 79:11).

"And God raised the Lord and will also raise us up by his power" (1 Cor. 6:14).

"For he was crucified in weakness, but lives by the power of God. For we also are weak in him, but in dealing with you we will live with him by the power of God" (2 Cor. 13:4).

"With a strong hand and an outstretched arm, for his steadfast love endures forever" (Ps. 136:12).

"But Jesus looked at them and said, 'With man this is impossible, but with God all things are possible'" (Matt. 19:26).

"It is he who made the earth by his power, who established the world by his wisdom, and by his understanding stretched out the heavens" (Jer. 10:12).

Suffering in Our World Today

At five years old, a vibrant little girl called McKenna Claire got what her parents thought was the flu. After taking her to see their doctor, they were sent immediately to the Children's Hospital of Orange County where McKenna was hooked up to monitors and an I.V., and they were told they would have to spend the night in order to have an MRI the next morning. Then came the longest wait of their lives. When doctors finally came to give them the diagnosis, it was worse than they could have ever imagined. Not only did McKenna have brain cancer, but she had the worst kind possible: Diffuse Intrinsic Pontine Glioma (DIPG). The doctors told them that children do not survive this cancer and that they could expect to have only 9 to 18 months with their daughter. With radiation and a clinical trial of oral chemotherapy, the doctors would be able to reverse some of the effects of the tumor for a short time. However, after an exhaustive search of the best institutions in the country, McKenna's parents realized that there was no cure.

Mid-morning on July 21, six months after her initial diagnosis, McKenna's breathing pattern changed. Her doctor confirmed they were losing her. Strong until the end, McKenna managed to wait until all of her family could give her one last kiss and say goodbye. Around noon, held by her mother and surrounded by her family and friends, she took her last breath. McKenna lost her battle exactly two weeks shy of her eighth birthday.[1]

God's Power and Suffering

When we look at the awful situations that some men, women, and children have to face, we can't help but look to God and say, "Where are you?" If God is good, powerful, and strong, then why do tragedies happen? If God is so powerful, why did we have to have a funeral service for five Dallas, Texas police officers? Why did officer Chad Vanden Berg, a local Los Angeles County Deputy Sheriff, have to lie in a hospital bed fighting for his life after being gunned down on the streets? I am certain some of you have had to endure hardships in your past, and some are in the midst of a storm right now. If God is good and powerful, why is there suffering? We could have this discussion on a philosophical level or an intellectual level, but the truth is, we've probably all battled some form of suffering in real life. We ask questions such as these: Why couldn't God stop my parents from getting a divorce? Why did my child have to die? Why did child abuse happen in a home where I should've been protected and secure? Why did my loved one get cancer? What God is worth worshiping who would let my daughter suffer and die from brain cancer?

There are no easy answers to these questions, and they raise some troubling questions about God. Is God powerless? Can he not do anything about our suffering? Is

God indifferent? Is he detached? Or worse yet, does God *cause* some of our troubles? I think deep down we wonder, "Why didn't God create a world with no tragedy or suffering?" If we created the world, we'd probably make the world a bit different. If we created the world, only good things would happen. If we were God, good kids would get straight As. Faithful spouses would have fairytale marriages. Lonely people would have great friends. Good parents would never get cancer. Couples who wanted to have children would have as many as they wanted. And the Dodgers would win the World Series year after year. That's how it would be if we were in charge of the world, right?

So why didn't God create a world in which everything was only good all the time? The short answer is . . . he did! Genesis 1:31 says: *"And God saw everything that he had made, and behold, it was very good."* There was no suffering, no tragedy, no cancer. He saw the world he made, and it was awesome. So if God is not the author of suffering and tragedy, where do suffering and tragedy come from?

Sometimes, tragedy is the result of our own sin. It's the law of natural consequences. If I cheat on my spouse, I'm going to have poor relationships. If I drink too much and eat the wrong foods, it's no wonder that I have some health issues. If I'm a workaholic and unengaged with my kids, it's no wonder they reject me.

Some tragedy is the result of other people's sin. If you get carjacked at a shopping center, that's someone else's sin. If your mate is abusive or if your parents divorce, that's suffering caused by somebody else's sin.

Some tragedy is the result of Satan's attacks. Satan is not in charge, and he's not in control of this world. The Bible tells us that Satan came to steal, kill, and destroy (John 10:10). Job suffered bankruptcy and the death of all 10 of his children, and he also suffered a great deal physically. This wasn't because of his sin or other people's sin. He suffered these things because Satan was attacking him.

Mostly, tragedy happens because we live in a fallen world. Ever since Adam and Eve allowed sin to enter God's perfect world, we've seen tragedy and suffering—things like droughts and famine, fires, hurricanes, tornadoes, and viruses. The water is polluted, and the air is contaminated. When sin came into the world, the system became unbalanced. Paul describes it as the birth pains leading up to the return of Jesus (Matt. 24:8).

God doesn't cause evil, but he does permit it in the world. Rain falls on the just and the unjust. Jesus acknowledges this in John 16:33, *"In this world you will have trouble."* God created a world free from suffering and pain and tragedy, but he also created a world of free will. In our fallen state, that free will leads to sin and destruction. So then, why did God allow free will? Because God is love and real love always has a choice. We see that in our relationships. I'm glad my wife loves me, not because God computer programmed her to love me. She chooses to love me, and that means a lot.

Knowing that we would suffer, why did God create the world? For the same reason we have kids. We know that our kids are going to face trouble and have hurts, disappointments, failure, and hardships in life, but we created them anyhow. We took the risk because we also knew there was a potential for joy, love, and relationship. The same is true for God. The truth is, simply understanding where tragedy and suffering come from doesn't help us much. One of the biggest mistakes is thinking that there is an answer that will help our pain go away. Even solid, rational answers can make some people feel insulted when they're going through a period of hardship, tragedy, and suffering. Is there a reason to hope? Is there a reason to keep hanging on? Where is our hope? Paul refers to a particular hope—a kind of *"hope that doesn't disappoint"* (Rom. 5:5). How do we find this hope? How can the story of hope become our story?

Job's Tragedy and Hope

There's a place in Scripture where God directly answers our question about hope. We find this in Job, *"In the land of Uz there lived a man whose name was Job. This man was blameless and upright; he feared God and shunned evil . . . He was the greatest man of all the people of the East"* (Job 1:1, 3b NIV). Job was the greatest man of all the people of the east. Job lived life right, yet a lot of bad things happened to him. He lost his family, wealth, servants, and health. And after all this, Job finally asked God, "Why?" I suppose that Job is asking "why" for all of us at some point. I'm sure we've all been in a "Why me, God?" situation and want to know the answer. For everyone who has experienced the pain of life, Job asks this question, and God answers:

Have you ever commanded the morning to appear and caused the dawn to rise in the east? Have you made daylight spread to the ends of the earth, to bring an end to the night's wickedness? . . . Do you know where the gates of death are located? Have you seen the gates of utter gloom? Do you realize the extent of the earth? Tell me about it if you know. Where does light come from, and where does darkness go? Can you take each to its home? Do you know how to get there? But of course you know all this! For you were born before it was all created, and you are so very experienced!

Job 38:12–13, 17–21 NLT

Then Job finally gets to answer God, *"I am nothing — how could I ever find the answers? I will cover my mouth with my hand. I have said too much already. I have nothing more to say"* (Job 40:4–5 NLT). In effect, God tells Job: I know, you don't. I understand, you don't. I see what you don't see. I'm God, you're not, and there's your answer.

It is easy to read this and think that God is being cold here, but that is not an accurate picture of God. As human beings, we are limited in our understanding of God. He always has existed and will continue to exist; he is all-knowing; he is everywhere at once, and he is all-powerful. Because we don't share those qualities with God, we can never understand everything there is to know about him and all that he is doing. In some strange way, that knowledge comforts me. I find hope in that. God had a plan to use Job's life, and his life is a reminder to me that God's ways are better than my ways.

Koby Gets Hurt

My son, Koby, was four years old and running around the house. It was December and my wife was at a Christmas party for work. So it was just me and the kids. We were playing all evening, having a good time, and it was finally time for bed. Koby took one last sprint around the corner to turn into his room and slipped, hitting his mouth on the end table and splitting his lip open. I grabbed him, and there was blood all over. I looked at his lip and knew it needed stitches. When I told this little four-year-old that we needed to go to the ER to have the doctor look at it, his demeanor quickly turned to worry. It was difficult for me to explain why his loving daddy would take him to a place where a doctor would poke a needle through his flesh. Even though I wasn't the one doing it, I was the one allowing it. I found myself saying a few things to comfort Koby that night as we drove to the emergency room, and maybe God wants to say something like this to you today.

#1 You Are Not Alone.

I kept telling Koby that I would not leave him, that I would be with him the entire time, and that I would go into the room with him while the doctor stitched him up.

There is a story about three men in the Old Testament named Shadrach, Meshach, and Abednego. They refused to bow down to an idol and were punished by being thrown into a blazing furnace. Here is what happened to while they were in the fire.

But suddenly, Nebuchadnezzar jumped up in amazement and exclaimed to his advisers, "Didn't we tie up three men and throw them into the furnace?" "Yes, Your Majesty, we certainly did," they replied. "Look!" Nebuchadnezzar shouted. "I see four men, unbound, walking around in the fire unharmed! And the fourth looks like a god!"

Dan. 3:24–25 NLT

God was with them; God did not leave Shadrach, Meshach, and Abednego alone! Jesus said:

I will not leave you as orphans; I will come to you. Yet a little while and the world will see me no more, but you will see me. Because I live, you also will live. In that day you will know that I am in my Father, and you in me, and I in you. Whoever has my commandments and keeps them, he it is who loves me. And he who loves me will be loved by my Father, and I will love him and manifest myself to him.

John 14:18–21

Have you ever watched somebody go through a horrible experience in their life and thought, I could never go through what they're going through? I couldn't survive it . . . I couldn't handle it. If my baby died, I don't think I could make it. If my wife were diagnosed with cancer, I'd be inconsolable. If I lost my health or my job, life would be over for me. And yet, I could tell you story after story after story of Jesus's followers in our church who found the strength when they needed it. When they thought they couldn't take another step, they did. When they needed God the most, he was with them in that moment to give them the strength that only God, through his Holy Spirit, can give.

Remember, when you're standing at the casket of someone that you love, God is with you. If you find yourself sitting in the waiting room at the hospital awaiting news, God is with you, and you are not alone. He not only goes through the fire with you, but he keeps his hand on the thermostat.

#2 I Know How You Feel.

When I was waiting with Koby in the ER waiting room, I told him that I knew exactly how he felt. I looked at Koby and told him, "Been there, done that." Hebrews 4:15 tells us that we have a God who sympathizes with us and that we can boldly approach him with our concerns in time of need. Sometimes, the answer we're looking for in our deepest struggles is not an explanation, but an incarnation. Knowing that Jesus came into our world and experienced exactly what we experience brings comfort. Nobody has lived out more goodness than Jesus. Nobody experienced more evil and bad than Jesus. We have a God who lived in our world, and he can genuinely say, "I know how you feel." Jesus skinned his knees, he got his feelings hurt, he felt hunger and thirst, he was tired, and he suffered, even to the point of death. Hear this: When you hurt, he hurts.

#3 Your Pain Has a Purpose.

As we sat in the waiting room for what felt like forever, Koby's nervousness was apparent. I tried to explain to him that his pain had a purpose. I told him the story of the Shaws, a couple who had a baby born with Down Syndrome. Shortly after the birth of their child when the situation became known, a number of people got together to pray for the Shaws. The prayers started out like this: "Be with the Shaws during this sad time. Be with them during this tragedy. God, we don't understand why." People took turns praying in this way, until it came to another person. This man had a teenage son, Jimmy, who had Down Syndrome. And his prayer was a little different. He prayed, "God, I thank you for the joy that can now come into this home that they would never have known without the birth of this special child." You see, he knew that pain has a purpose. And that God works all things together for good. Many of us can say it was through a season of pain that we were drawn back to God and into a real relationship with Jesus. As it says in 2 Corinthians 7:10, *"For the kind of sorrow God wants us to experience leads us away from sin and results in salvation. There's no regret for that kind of sorrow"* (NLT).

That's a pretty radical thought, isn't it? That we will never regret the sorrow that comes our way in life. Why? Because if God can use our sorrow to help us seek him and if the sorrow helps us to find God, the value of that experience is so great. Whatever pain we experienced in the first place makes the result so much greater. Like a loving father who allows his child to get a painful shot in his lip, followed by a needle poking him several times to put in five stitches, God allows pain because it's for our greater good. And maybe God allows cancer to teach us to value what is eternal. And maybe God allows the difficult boss to teach us self-control. And maybe God allows unemployment to teach us faith. And maybe God allows us to have a baby that sleeps all day and is awake all night to teach us patience. He doesn't cause all these things, but he does work them together for good, and he never wastes a hurt.

When the nurses called us back into the room to be treated, the reality of the situation was clear in Koby's eyes. As we walked back, Koby grabbed on to me tightly and laid his little head on my shoulder. And his response was the best response that we can have when we're going through tragedy and suffering—he held on to me tightly.

#4 Hang onto Your Heavenly Father and Don't Let Go.

Hanging on is what Habakkuk did. He lived in an agricultural society and, in Habakkuk 3, he describes a scene of total devastation around him. He's disappointed and frustrated, and nothing is turning out the way that he wants.

> *Though the fig tree should not blossom, nor fruit be on the vines, the produce of the olive fail and the fields yield no food, the flock be cut off from the fold and there be no herd in the stalls, yet I will rejoice in the Lord; I will take joy in the God of my salvation. God, the Lord, is my strength.*
>
> Hab. 3:17–19

We might say, "though I'm unemployed, though my child is sick, though my marriage is struggling, though my health is failing, though everything in my life is a mess, though my kids are far from God . . . nevertheless, I will rejoice in the Lord; God is my strength." When the vines are empty and the fields are barren, hang on to God and don't let go.

There's one last thing that I told Koby as he was experiencing so much pain that night. As the doctors and nurses gave him a shot right in the cut on his lip to numb the pain, he looked at me with worried eyes, and I told him that the pain would end soon.

#5 The Pain Will Be over Soon.

And in the middle of that process, I told him that we would stop and get Golden Spoon when we were done there. And strangely, of all the things that I said that night, that was the one message that had the most impact. It was something for him to look forward to.

Shifting Winds

As Acts 1 begins, the disciples are on a high because Jesus has been resurrected, and they are now with the guy who defeated death. Jesus gave them some instructions (Acts 1:8). He told them that they would be used to spread the word of the gospel to the world. Jesus told them that he was going to use their lives and the story of the gospel for the rest of the world. And that had to be exhilarating. "God's going to use us . . . how cool!" And then the winds shifted, and Jesus disappeared from them (Acts 1:9). The disciples had been with him for three years, 24 hours a day. And now he's gone . . . vanished . . . ascended into heaven. Talk about shifting winds. What they knew as their life was no longer the same because the winds shifted, and they were scared. The cord had been cut.

Then something dramatic happened. *"And suddenly there came from heaven a sound like a mighty rushing wind, and it filled the entire house where they were sitting"* (Acts 2:2). A wind came through and launched a new era. The rest of Acts talks about a spiritual revival, and the church that we serve today was established. When the wind shifts, God can do a new thing. It's interesting to study how the word *wind* is used. The wind almost always comes when God ushers in a new and better era.

Think about the story of Noah. Noah and his family were in the ark with all the animals for 40 days and 40 nights. God remembered Noah and his family (Gen. 8:1). The wind shifted, the water went away, and the entire world was made new. God did a new thing in Noah's life and in the entire world.

Remember the story of Moses and the Israelites who escaped from Egypt. They were chased by the Egyptians and trapped by the Red Sea.

> *Then Moses stretched out his hand over the sea, and all that night the Lord drove the sea back with a strong east wind and turned it into dry land. The waters were divided, and the Israelites went through the sea on dry ground, with a wall of water on their right and on their left.*
>
> Exod. 14:21-22 NIV

God was able to do a new thing with the Israelites.

Hope amidst Tragedy

How can we bring all of this full circle? Remember the opening story about McKenna Claire? When McKenna died, her mother and father, Dave and Kristine Wetzel, arranged for her brain tumor tissue (along with her brain and spinal cord) to be donated to researchers at Stanford University who are on the cutting edge of pediatric brain cancer and DIPG research.

To this day, the Wetzels work tirelessly to raise money to help keep McKenna's tumor growing. The very thing that killed their daughter is the very thing they work so hard to keep alive. They've started a foundation and work to send her tumor to researchers all over the world to conduct studies.

Conclusion

So, where is God in our suffering? Where is God when our lives are devastated by some tragic situation? The book of Job doesn't deny suffering. McKenna Claire and her family certainly suffered, and many of you reading this have suffered or will one day suffer. I am comforted that God is with us when we suffer. In the story of Job, God didn't abandon him in his suffering. And like McKenna's story, God has a purpose for our suffering. McKenna Claire's story is very similar to the gospel story of Jesus Christ. Consider for a moment that God created this beautiful young girl, not to live the American dream, but to have a far greater impact on the world.

Because of McKenna Claire's life, death, and the donation of her brain tumor tissue, there is the hope that one day, many will be saved from this horrible disease. Not everyone will suffer to the same degree as Job or McKenna, and our suffering may not be the beginning of a wonderful foundation like the McKenna Claire Foundation. But our suffering can serve to bless countless lives. Our suffering can have an eternal effect on someone's life when we allow God to use it to point people to Jesus, who suffered—undeservedly—more than anyone who has ever walked on the earth. But this was his purpose. God's purpose for his son was to allow him to suffer, but he did it so we can live. God has a purpose for our suffering. Be comforted in knowing he will not abandon you in your suffering; he will care for us, and he will remind us of our place in his kingdom while we are going through it. Jesus willingly suffered so that anyone who repents of their sin can come to him in faith, be forgiven, and receive eternal life in a kingdom where he will wipe away every tear. Death shall be no more, cancer will be no more, suffering will be no more. There will be no more mourning, crying, or pain. Ten thousand years into eternity, the suffering in this life won't compare to the glory that we will be experiencing as fully redeemed children of the King![2] To that I say, come Lord Jesus, come.

NOTES

Chapter 1

1. Trevin Wax, *Counterfeit Gospels: Rediscovering the Good News in a World of False Hope* (Chicago: Moody Publishers, 2011), Google Books.

2. Tripp, *New Morning Mercies: A Daily Gospel Devotional* (Wheaton, Illinois: Crossway, 2014), 31.

3. Ibid.

4. Rick Warren, *Daily Devotions: Day 7. Transformed: How God Changes Us* (Rancho Santa Margarita, CA: Saddleback Church, 2014).

Chapter 2

1. National Institute on Alcohol Abuse and Alcoholism, U.S. Department of Health and Human Services, "Alcohol Facts and Statistics," https://www.niaaa.nih.gov/alcohol-health/overview-alcohol-consumption/alcohol-facts-and-statistics.

Chapter 4

1. Kathryn A. London, "Cohabitation, Marriage, Marital Dissolution, and Remarriage: United States, 1988: Data From the National Survey of Family Growth," *PsycEXTRA Dataset* (1991), doi:10.1037/e608662007-001.

2. Gary Chapman, *The Five Love Languages: How to Express Heartfelt Commitment to Your Mate* (Chicago, IL: Moody Publishers, 2004).

Chapter 5

1. R. Kent Hughes, *Preaching the Word* (Wheaton, IL: Crossway Books, 1989).

2. Preston Sprinkle, "The Gospel Alliance Gathering" (Dyer, IN, Faith Church, September 12, 2017).

Chapter 6

1. Harvey Turner, *Friend of Sinners: An Approach to Evangelism* (Houston, TX: Lucid, 2016), 31.

2. Jim Carrey, "*The Majestic* Interview," interview by Heather Wadowski, December 26, 2001, www.jimcarreyonline.com/recent/news.php?id=496.

Chapter 7

1. Tom Mercer, *8 to 15: The World Is Smaller Than You Think* (Victorville, CA: Oikos Books, 2013).

Chapter 9

1. McKenna Claire Foundation, "Macky's Story," accessed August 11, 2017, http://mckennaclairefoundation. org/about/mackys-story.

2. Paul David Tripp, "Wednesday's Word," accessed September 7, 2017, https://www.paultripp.com/wednes days-word?mc_cid=4c4fd3a44c&mc_eid=a76cbbc9a2.

CPSIA information can be obtained
at www.ICGtesting.com
Printed in the USA
FSOW03n0615310118
43867FS